Grace Paley

Illuminating the Dark Lives

Jacqueline Taylor

Grace Paley

Illuminating the Dark Lives

University of Texas Press, Austin

Copyright © 1990 by the University of Texas Press
All rights reserved
Printed in the United States of America

First Edition, 1990

Requests for permission to reproduce material from this work
should be sent to Permissions, University of Texas Press, Box
7819, Austin, Texas 78713-7819.

⊛ The paper used in this publication meets the minimum
requirements of American National Standard for Information
Sciences—Permanence of Paper for Printed Library Materials,
ANSI Z39.48-1984.

LIBRARY OF CONGRESS CATALOGING-IN-PUBLICATION DATA
Taylor, Jacqueline.
  Grace Paley : illuminating the dark lives / by Jacqueline
  Taylor.
  —1st ed.
      p.   cm.
  Includes bibliographical references.
  ISBN 0-292-79055-4 (alk. paper).
    1. Paley, Grace—Criticism and interpretation.   2. Paley,
  Grace—Characters—Women.   3. Women in literature.
    I. Title.
PS3566.A46Z89   1990
813'.54—dc20   89- 39704
                                                        CIP

For Carol

Contents

Preface

If this book had a single beginning, it was a chamber theatre production of five Grace Paley short stories that I directed at DePaul University in 1985. As I worked with my cast and crew on that show, I became increasingly intrigued by Paley's innovative narrative techniques. So, my first thanks go to the students who worked with me on that show, especially Ken Beider, Pattey Cook, and Pamela Schroeder. Two years later, Mary Argianas and Mitra Emad performed two Paley short stories for another chamber theatre production, and again I learned about Paley from directing them in their performances. I first worked out some of the language issues explored here with my gender and communication class in 1986 and have discussed Paley, language, narrative structure, and mutedness with some eight other classes since then. I am indebted to the many DePaul students who have helped me develop these ideas.

Many friends and colleagues around the country contributed support, encouragement, criticism, and ideas. Several of these must have special thanks. Joanne Devine read the manuscript in various stages, offering helpful comments and bibliographic information. She has been a source of encouragement, ideas, and information since I first became interested in questions of language and gender. Lynn Christine Miller read and commented on an earlier version. Carol Cyganowski read a draft of the entire manuscript with enormous dispatch and then helped me to see what I needed to do to get the project into its final form. My book group, Marla Cass, Diane Krall, Miriam Pickus, Carol Sadtler, Susan Schleef, Elaine Stocker, and Sandra Whisler, made the manuscript the topic of one month's discussion. Their interest and comments helped me to keep faith in the project and refine my ideas. They also served as the collective model for the intelligent, well-read, feminist, nonacademic reader whom I hoped would form part of the audience for this book. Kristin Langellier read and commented on the section that traces the connection between Paley's stories and women's personal narratives, a section that was inspired by Langellier's own work. My two reviewers for University of Texas Press made a number of suggestions that strengthened the book. Frankie Westbrook, my editor, along with the rest of the staff at U.T. Press, has made publishing this book easier than I had any reason to expect it could be. After Marjorie Piechowski helped me to put together grant proposals seeking support for this work, Paul H. Gray, Beverly Whitaker Long, James Malek, Jean Haskell Speer, and Carol Simpson Stern wrote in support of those proposals. DePaul University gave me a one-year research leave and summer support while I wrote. The National Endowment for the Humanities provided me with a summer stipend. Mitra Emad helped with the final tasks of proofreading and indexing. My parents, Eldred and Marjorie Taylor, contributed, as always, their collosal faith in me. At the end, Lucia Taylor gave me the happiest of reasons to hurry up and get it done. Throughout this project, Carol Sadtler talked with me about these ideas, read multiple versions, made suggestions, and took my work seriously (without ever losing her sense of humor). Writing this book would not have been nearly as much fun without her.

Finally, I owe a debt to Grace Paley. When I called up without an introduction and wanted an interview, she agreed to talk to me about her work. She was generous with her time and patient with my inexperienced approach to interviewing. But more than that, I thank her for these stories, which have given me so many happy hours of reading and study.

Grace Paley

Illuminating the Dark Lives

Introduction

In a world where women's voices have been routinely silenced, Grace Paley dares to create a voice that is boldly female. In her three volumes of short stories, Paley manifests a willingness to speak the unspeakable: she is irreverent, comic, compassionate, and wise. Critics have regularly remarked on the distinctiveness of this voice; Paley is an innovator, and her innovations often occur in relationship to the particularly female consciousness she articulates.

Paley reports that she began writing fiction because she was "thinking an awful lot about women's lives" and "wasn't able to get it into poems."[1] Convinced that women's lives were "common and important," she created her first stories out of a desire to understand and record the lives of the women around her.[2] Her first short story collection, *The Little Disturbances of Man: Stories of Women and Men at Love* (1959), reveals a sensitivity to women and a woman-centered consciousness remarkable for the tradition-bound decade of the fifties. *Enormous Changes at the Last Minute* (1974) and *Later the Same Day* (1985) continue this concern with the lives of ordinary women, while adding to Paley's achievement as an innovator in language and subject matter.

On the strength of three slim volumes of short stories containing only forty-five stories, Paley has earned a reputation as a writer's writer. Written in colloquial language, her stories are deceptively simple; they can seem at first glance to be uncomplicated and even unadorned tales, but closer inspection reveals their careful craft.

Again and again reviewers and other authors describe her as one of a kind, an original, unique.

Paley's work is distinctive for a number of reasons. In the first place, her subject matter is mundane. She peoples her stories with the diverse and ordinary residents of Greenwich Village. Ignoring the heroic and dramatic, she gives her particular attention instead to what she calls "ordinary people [who] just lead unpowerful, ordinary, hopeful lives"[3]—women and children in such everyday settings as the playground, the kitchen, and the grocery store; welfare mothers; parents in a retirement home; women and men living together in the "homey life" of middle age. The ethnic and racial mix of her characters adds to our sense that we are hearing stories often excluded from the concerns of dominant literature: Jewish, Irish Catholic, Puerto Rican, African American, and Asian voices all have their say. Another distinguishing characteristic of Paley's literature is the comic voice that pervades her work. She writes about the ordinary trials and tragedies that touch the human heart with a wisecracking humor that refuses bathos. The edge of that humor never turns on the powerless. Although the wisecracks and smart remarks are relentless, she somehow manages to create a world in which women are not the butt of the joke. This brings us to a third distinguishing characteristic. Paley writes as a feminist, and her brand of feminism is one that includes resistance to all forms of oppression: "I see feminism as an analysis that sees the world in terms of domination, by one class, by one sex, by one tree (laughter). No that's a joke, but if you watch the woods, you get very annoyed at certain trees, I'll tell you that (laughter)."[4] Paley's fiction maintains an insistent awareness of the systems of oppression that silence minorities, reminding the reader again and again of the difficulty of really listening to the voice of the other. This vision of feminism results in her refusal to keep politics out of her fictive world; instead she creates characters who live and work with the awareness that nuclear annihilation is a constant threat and danger and "starting now, it had better interfere with any daily pleasure" ("Anxiety," *LD,* 101).[5] Yet even as she looks unsentimentally at the loss and dislocation of modern life, she achieves a fiction permeated with joy "because of the possible happy ending."[6]

Beyond all these distinguishing characteristics, however, Paley's language has attracted attention as the chief source of her originality. Her stories make brilliantly inventive use of semantic and narrative structure. Reviewers consistently remark on a language that is "uniquely her own" and a voice that is "the defining characteristic of her art."[7] She writes in dialogue with and often in defiance of the semantic and narrative conventions that constrain all writers.

The daughter of Russian Jewish immigrants, Paley grew up in a language-rich environment that no doubt contributed to her ability to place words in fresh and lively contexts: "For the eventual making of literature, that early life was probably healthy—lots of women in the kitchen talking, two strong languages, English and Russian in my ear at home, and the language of my grandmother and the grownups in the street—Yiddish—to remind me of the person I really was, the middle-class child of working people, the comfortable daughter of hounded wanderers, resting for a generation between languages."[8]

Despite widespread acknowledgment of Paley's originality, critics have seemed at a loss to account for the power of her work. Her published volumes are widely reviewed and often acclaimed, and she regularly appears in literary anthologies, but she has attracted little scholarly attention. This is due in part, no doubt, to her relatively slight output and the simple fact that short stories rarely receive the critical attention accorded to novels and poetry. But a more important reason for the critical silence toward Paley's work is that her writing does not fit readily into the established literary frameworks. Somewhat too innovative to conform to the conventions of realistic and mimetic fiction, she nevertheless shares little with the modernists and metafictionists. The French journal *Delta* makes Paley the subject of a rare special issue; in its introduction, editor Kathleen Hulley reports on the difficulty of soliciting manuscripts: "A number of critics who originally offered to write something for this collection eventually gave it up, complaining, 'I can't find anything to say,' 'she is too experimental,' or 'not experimental enough.' 'There is no theoretical handle to grasp.' Above all was the complaint, 'she is too direct, she leaves me with nothing to say. Paley has no secrets: she tells what she is doing.'"[9]

This study rests on the proposition that Paley's fiction voices a distinctly woman-centered point of view and in so doing validates an experience and a perspective that have been muted in our language and our literature. The reviewers are accurate in their assessment that language is central to the originality of Paley's work. But crucial to an appreciation of what makes her language innovative is an understanding of its relationship to the language of male dominance. She has stories to tell that cannot be accommodated by the dominant discourse; thus, the process of creating language that *can* contain her stories is a significant part of Paley's enterprise. By creating words, definitions, and narrative strategies she opens up a space in the dominant discourse for stories that otherwise would be suppressed. The result of all this is a powerful contribution to the development of a woman-centered language and literature and, by extension, the construction of a social world in which woman-centered meanings can flourish.

Dominant meanings silence women by convincing us that we have nothing to say worth hearing. Paley's own development as a writer illustrates this. In an interview with Kathleen Hulley, Paley describes how difficult it was for her to believe that women's lives could serve as interesting subjects for literature:

> GP: For a long time I thought women's lives . . . I didn't think I
> was shit, but I really thought my life as a woman was shit.
> Who could be interested in this crap? I was very interested in
> it, but I didn't have enough social ego to put it down. I had to
> develop that to a point where I said, "I don't give a damn."
> Women who have thought their lives were boring have found
> they're interesting to one another.
>
> KH: Is that part of what you meant when you said something about
> your stories taking what is dark and hidden and recreating a
> balance in the world?
>
> GP: Something like that. Stories illuminate. That's the purpose of a
> story for me. To shine a light on what's dark and give it light.
> And the balance is something else. . . . It's justice.
>
> KH: What are you most interested in balancing?
>
> GP: The dark lives of women. This is what made me write to begin
> with. And at the time I thought no one would be interested in
> seeing it. But I had to illuminate it anyway. If for nobody else,
> for myself and my friends.[10]

Paley's discussion serves as a testimonial to the power of the dominant culture to define and limit the stories we believe we can tell. But it simultaneously bears witness to the power of women to transcend and transform the language. Paley maintains that if "something's been written, and I've already read it, I tend not to need to write about it myself. I write stories that I need to hear."[11] It is precisely this need to explore and illuminate what has been hidden (or silenced) that has brought Paley to the kind of transforming language this book explores.

Muted Group Theory

Feminist critics have provided overwhelming evidence that the language we speak places women at a disadvantage. Reflecting the social world, language is male dominated. At least two women have felt strongly enough about the male bias in language to invent names that make the point: Dale Spender speaks of "man made language"[12] and Varda One coined the term "manglish."[13]

Despite the fact that a male-dominated language constrains women, we are bound to language, for how else can we articulate the problem except through the very language that imprisons us? Adrienne Rich expresses this precisely when she says, "This is the oppressor's language/ yet I need it to talk to you."[14]

The muted group theory developed by anthropologist Edwin Ardener and elaborated by Shirley Ardener provides a useful framework for discussing Paley's transformative relationship to language.[15] This theory holds that although all humans participate at the unconscious level in the generation of ideas that order our experience, dominant (in our case, white, heterosexual, middle- or upper-class, male) members of society disproportionately control the forms or structures through which such consciousness can be articulated. As a result, language is particularly suited to expressing their experience and perspective. Consequently, women are at a disadvantage whenever we wish to express matters of particular concern to us. When speaking of experiences or perspectives that are uniquely (or at least more typically) female, we will encounter both language limitations and a reluctance among our listeners to attend to expressions that conflict with dominant concepts and meanings. If we wish to be heard, we find it necessary to express our ideas in "a form acceptable to men." This may lead women to an indirectness rather than a spontaneity of expression and may even impede our facility to bring to consciousness our unconscious thoughts.[16] In order to communicate through the dominant mode, women must engage in an act of translation, transforming "their own unconscious perceptions into such conscious ideas as will accord with those generated by the dominant group."[17] The muted group consequently "may be relatively more 'inarticulate' when expressing themselves through the idiom of the dominant group."[18] The term *muted* "recalls the muted sonority of a musical instrument—the sound different, tamped down, repressed, but still speaking, with the speech bearing the marks of partial silencing."[19]

Thus as women we find that we have experiences and perceptions which our language is not equipped to express. The lack of a suitable language impairs our ability to perceive such experiences clearly and accurately. An attempt to fit our experience to the dominant forms requires an act of translation and the risk of inarticulateness. If, in spite of all this, we do manage to perceive what we have no language for and invent the necessary language to express that perception, that expression is not likely to receive a proper hearing.

Of course, the fact that one group's perspective is muted in a culture does not mean that there is no possibility for articulating that perspective. Even when the language does not provide suitable words and phrases for expressing particular ideas, speakers have proved infinitely resourceful at generating new ways of speaking. As long as the experiences exist, the potential for developing adequate expression exists. Yet it is not hard to see that if we had to develop new language each time we had an experience we wished to communicate, communication would be seriously impeded and much would go unspoken.

Nor is there any assurance that articulating a perspective will guarantee a hearing. Both Tillie Olsen and Joanna Russ have provided powerful critiques of the ways in which women writers are discouraged or prevented from writing in the first place, and in the second place minimized, ridiculed, and discounted if we do manage to overcome the obstacles that would prevent us from getting our words into print.[20]

The forces that silence women include robbing women of the kind of life that can lead to finding a voice by denying education (the majority of the world's illiterates are women[21]) and the opportunity to earn a living above the poverty level,[22] ignoring what women say, commenting on the unintelligibility of women, and describing the experiences of over half of the world's population as narrow and lacking in universality. Women can speak if we must, but if we are not recognized as possible authors of perception, what we say scarcely merits attention.[23]

Despite all the problems mutedness poses for women and other marginalized groups, it also carries with it a source of strength and the potential for its own deconstruction. For the dominant group sees only the reality it describes and takes that to be the whole of reality, but muted groups necessarily recognize that the dominant perspective is only one among many. The relationship of the dominant and muted groups has been depicted by Ardener through a diagram of two almost overlapping circles. The overlap describes the reality known through experience by both. Elaine Showalter explains: "women know what the male crescent is like, even if they have never seen it, because it becomes the subject of legend (like the wilderness). But men do not know what is in the wild."[24] Muted groups have ready access to the realization that their world view is a partial one, for they are constantly confronted with a dominant reality that differs from their lived experience. In fact, women "oscillate between the two parts of the circle that represents them, between difference and dominance."[25] This double view (double-consciousness)[26] offers a powerful corrective to the dangers of egocentrism and solipsism.

Breaking Silence

The perpetuation of women's mutedness depends on the willingness of women to describe our experience only in the words and categories available to us from the dominant culture, a willingness that has become increasingly problematic in the current wave of feminism. As soon as women begin to articulate a woman-centered perspective, we begin to move away from our strictly muted state. Dale Spender explains: "This is a dialectic process. There will not necessarily be any redistribution of male defined power—legal, political, educational, etc.—simply because women cease to be silent, but neither will there be a redistribution of power if women remain silent. As women cease to be muted, male supremacy becomes problematic; as it becomes problematic, women receive more encouragement to break their silence."[27] Calls to break silence have become commonplace in feminist writing.[28]

The transformation of literature and the transformation of life are inextricably linked in the views of those who join with Adrienne Rich in her call for "a whole new poetry beginning here."[29] A story told by Cynthia Enloe aptly describes the scope of the project that such language change envisions: "I remember, several years ago, a 'Take Back the Night' march. We were making our way towards the Fenway chanting 'take back the night,' when Pam Chamberlain stopped and said, 'Wait, I've got it—take back everything.' I've always remembered Pam—why think so modestly? What I want us to do is take back the meaning of everything, to expand the boundaries of what feminists can think about as feminists."[30]

This coming to free and woman-centered speech, this beginning the process of taking back everything, marks a new era in women's language and literature. The deliberate articulation of the muted reveals a radical shift in consciousness. Rachel Blau DuPlessis notes that "giving voice to the voiceless and making visible the invisible are two prime maneuvers in feminist poetics."[31] And according to Alicia Suskin Ostriker, "One of the ways we recognize that a woman writer has taken some kind of liberating jump is that her muted parts begin to explain themselves."[32]

Paley's Challenge to Mutedness

It is in this spirit of investigating what happens when women begin to articulate the muted that we turn to an examination of the short stories of Grace Paley. All of us, each time we speak, participate in the creation of our common language. Only in the last two decades, however, have large numbers of women "collectively attempted to repossess"[33] this language that has so often been used to exclude us. Repossessing language changes not only the face of literature but our perception and vision of the world. Grace Paley is one of a growing number of women who through some sort of liberating leap of consciousness have found the means to write the unwritable. By attending to her bold voice, we can begin to learn what a free woman might sound like.

The rest of this book is devoted to the proposition that the short stories of Grace Paley provide a valuable example of free and woman-centered writing. Refusing mutedness and the denials and distortions of dominant language, Paley claims the power to repossess language and subvert conventional forms. Her linguistic innovations fall into two major categories: semantic encoding and narrative structures. Chapters 1 through 3 concentrate on semantic issues.

As a feminist, Paley has developed an increasingly critical stance toward dominant language. The first chapter, "This Narrow Language," traces the development of Paley's conscious recognition of the problems women encounter when trying to use a language based on male categories and meanings. Her fiction contains numerous examples of women objecting to the inadequate meanings of the dominant language.

Chapter 2, "Illuminating the Dark Lives of Women," argues that dominant definitions result in four categories of semantic denials and distortions: androcentric language, exclusionist language, partial language, and absolute denials. Paley's innovative and subversive strategies challenge dominant language in all four categories.

Humor is basic to Paley's redefinitions. Chapter 3, "What Is There to Laugh?" analyzes her use of the comic impulse to construct a woman-centered perspective. Paley's characteristically irreverent humor is built on wordplay that occurs in the space between dominant and woman-centered meanings. Earthiness and optimism fuel her comic stance, while Jewish humor provides a survivalist model for humor as the source of a radical critique of dominance.

To tell the stories she thinks are important, Paley revises and invents not only words and definitions but narrative structure as well. Chapter 4, "Not Necessarily the End," examines Paley's resistance to narrative beginning, middle, and end. The short story "A Conversation with My Father" discusses overtly a resistance that is evident throughout her corpus. Paley's subversive strategies include not only the development of plots that exist outside the traditional resolutions for female protagonists in either marriage or death but also the creation of texts that elude closure and fixity.

Chapter 5, "As Simply as Possible," considers links between Paley's work and women's oral tradition, particularly as manifested in personal narratives. For instance, critics have often faulted Paley for inadequate plot development, arguing that many of her stories do not really go anywhere. This same charge has also been leveled at women's personal narratives. Understanding that Paley draws strongly on a women's oral tradition makes possible a reassessment of some of the stories that reviewers have dismissed as weak.

The final chapter, "Voices from Who Knows Where," analyzes the strategies with which Paley undermines the authority and dominance of the narrator. These strategies include first-person narration, connections between the narrator and the reader, collective narration (as in a first-person plural point of view), identification with the other, contradictory first-person accounts, and, most radically, collaborative narration, a technique whereby narrators' versions of events are corrected and amended by the characters in the story. As characters and narrators collaborate in the telling of the story, they challenge the potentially solipsistic and monologic power of the narration. The result is a narrative technique that resists the privileging of any one point of view, insisting instead that any single version of events is limited and partial.

With a clear vision available to her in large part because of her marginal status, Paley subverts dominant assumptions and dominant language and speaks with a voice uniquely female and uniquely her own. The world she calls into being does not replace one partial vision with another but insists on the partiality of what any single one of us can see. She offers a model for a world transformed, for in her fiction anyone can be a storyteller and no one has the last word.

I
This Narrow Language

Don't you wish you could rise powerfully above your time and name? I'm sure we all try, but here we are, always slipping and falling down into them, speaking their narrow language.

—"THE STORY HEARER," *LD,* 140

With the publication of Paley's first collection of short stories, a boldly original voice emerged, telling stories about women unlike any we had heard before. But even though her early work challenges dominant meanings and offers woman-centered definitions, it does not provide the sort of explicit and conscious critique of male dominance in language that we find in her more recent work.

Of course, one can make changes in language without consciously identifying language as the site of a problem, and indeed Paley does so in her early work. But it is interesting that as Paley has matured, and as feminists have developed increasingly powerful critiques of the dominant language, Paley's stories have come to incorporate ever more explicit references to women's particularly problematic relationship with language. In arguing that Paley reveals a conscious awareness that women have been muted and offers specific challenges to examples of male dominance in language, this chapter will draw heavily on evidence in *Later the Same Day,* her most recent volume of short stories. But first I want to show that such language awareness, although much less consciously developed, is prefigured in her first two volumes.

When Paley began writing stories in the 1950s, the generic use of *man* and *he* went unchallenged, and no one voiced concern over the precedence of the male term in such phrases as "husband and wife" or "male and female." The title of Paley's first volume contains an interesting combination of accepting and challenging these evidences of male dominance which would provoke so much discussion twenty years later. *The Little Disturbances of Man: Stories of Women and Men at Love* is a title whose generic use of *man* sounds like a misnomer to contemporary ears. But the same title challenges dominant language in a subtitle that gives unconventional precedence to the female term. In fact, Paley's use of "women and men" was so unconventional that in the second edition of her book, a typesetter "inadvertently" transposed the words, a mistake Paley herself failed to catch.[1] The book continued to be printed with the transposed title until it was reissued in the eighties. The typesetter's mistake provides a dramatic illustration of the power of dominant meanings to reassert themselves.

The Little Disturbances of Man also contains the first evidence of Paley's belief that women and men do not always speak the same language. In "A Subject of Childhood," Faith's boyfriend Clifford accuses her of having done a "rotten job" as a mother and of raising her kids "lousy" and "stinking." These remarks so infuriate Faith that she hurls an ashtray at him. She takes this action because Clifford has used the wrong language: "'You don't say things like that to a woman,' I whispered. 'You damn stupid jackass. You just don't say anything like that to a woman. Wash yourself, moron, you're bleeding to death'" (140). "A Subject of Childhood" is one of two stories about Faith in this volume linked by the title "Two Short Sad Stories in a Long and Happy Life." Besides the characters of Faith and her two sons Richard and Anthony, these stories share a growing consciousness that women and men occupy different worlds (more on this in chapter 4). Faith's explanation to Clifford rests on the propositions that women have particular and distinctive language requirements and that men often fail to understand this.

The idea that sometimes women and men simply do not speak the same language surfaces again in Paley's second volume of stories:

> Cool it! he said. Come back. I was just starting to fuck you and you get so freaked.
> And another thing. Don't use that word. I hate it. When you're with a woman you have to use the language that's right for her.
> ("Enormous Changes at the Last Minute," *EC*, 128)

Paley's character is not the first to note that *fuck* is a word that describes sexual activity from a male perspective. As Germaine Greer noted in 1971, "All the vulgar linguistic emphasis is placed upon the *poking* element, *fucking, screwing, rooting, shagging* are all acts performed upon the passive female."[2]

Enormous Changes contains another instance of an explicit critique of male language. In "The Immigrant Story," Jack's use of dominant language seems to the female character so dangerous that she refuses to answer him. Jack and a woman friend (probably Faith) argue about why Jack as a young boy found his father sleeping in the crib. Jack shouts, "Bullshit! She was trying to make him feel guilty. Where were his balls?" The narrator-character explains to the reader: "I will never respond to that question. Asked in a worried way again and again, it may become responsible for the destruction of the entire world. I gave it two minutes of silence" (172). Never in the discussions of male dominance in language have we seen a clearer dissection of the word *balls* as a name for macho courage. This narrator knows she has encountered a word so dangerous that silence is the only effective response. A nuclear holocaust could be precipitated by just this mix of insecurity and machismo.

One other technique Paley has developed for critiquing male language appears in *Enormous Changes*. At times, she explicates the problems with dominant language by contrasting the dominant label with a woman's definition. A narrator who reflects the consciousness of Faith tells us about Faith's ex-husband, Ricardo:

> He was really, he said, a man's man. Like any true man's man, he ran after women too. . . .
>
>   He called them pet names, which generally referred to certain flaws in their appearance. He called Faith Baldy, although she is not and never will be bald. She is finehaired and fair, and regards it as part of the lightness of her general construction that when she gathers her hair into an ordinary topknot, the stuff escapes around the contour of her face, making her wisp-haired and easy to blush. He is now living with a shapely girl with white round arms he calls Fatty. ("Faith in the Afternoon," 34)

The contrast between Ricardo's and Faith's meanings in this scene is stark indeed. According to dominant meanings, a man's man is one whose masculinity is unassailable. He is unambiguously one of the boys. Faith's commentary on Ricardo's dominant definitions directs our attention to the objectifying and demeaning implications of his names for women. Ricardo's requisite pursuit of women depends on a view of women as interchangeable objects of male desire. Similarly, Ricardo's "pet names" are not endearments at all but call attention to the women's failure to conform to a narrowly defined and objectifying standard of female beauty.

Paley's critiques of and negotiations with dominant meanings depend on her belief that the meaning of a word is not absolutely fixed but rather is negotiated through use, a belief that surfaces in the title story of her second volume. In "Enormous Changes at the Last Minute," songwriter Dennis defends his use of a word (*ecology*) that Alexandra believes is too technical for a song: "Any word is good, it's the big word today anyway, said Dennis. It's what you do with the word. The language and the idea, they work it out together" (129). Dennis's comment recognizes that language and the ideas language represents are not identical but exist instead in a relationship of tension. Furthermore, meaning is evolutionary, negotiated through use.

Although language that is fixed and that represents perfectly the ideas to which it refers might simplify the world, it is not available to the narrator of another story in this collection, "Faith in a Tree": "Despite no education, Mrs. Finn always is more in charge of word meanings than I am. She is especially in charge of Good and Bad. My language limitations here are real. My vocabulary is adequate for writing notes and keeping journals but absolutely useless for an active moral life. If I really knew the language there would surely be in my head, as there is in Webster's or the *Dictionary of American Slang,* that unreducible verb designed to tell a person like me what to do next" (85). Although Faith claims that the language limitations are her own, the reader recognizes her ironic acknowledgment that Mrs. Finn, with her belief in absolutely fixed word meanings, has the more serious limitations. Faith shares with Paley a postmodern belief in the negotiation of meaning and the potential within language for the kind of wordplay that expands or revises definitions (we will examine the negotiation of meaning through wordplay more fully in the next chapter).

These first two collections of stories were published in 1959 and 1974. Thus, Paley wrote most of these stories well before the comprehensive critique of male dominance in language that feminists have recently articulated (in fact, many of these stories preceded the critique of male dominance at all—the word *sexism* was not coined until the late sixties).[3] Given the times in which she was writing, it is not surprising that these stories reveal relatively few examples of conscious critiques of language. As awareness of the male dominance revealed and perpetuated in language increased during the seventies, so too did Paley's explication of the problem in her stories. Her latest volume, *Later the Same Day,* provides ample evidence that Paley believes language is male dominated and language change worth the struggle.

The women in Paley's most recent stories recognize that many of the words used in the dominant language to name women function to demean or denigrate us. When the middle-aged Selena addresses her friends, she reveals a developing consciousness of this: "Well girls—excuse me, I mean ladies—it's time for me to rest" ("Friends," 76). Selena participates in the conscious language change which results from the recognition that naming grown women "girls" belittles them, but her substitution of "ladies" still smacks of patriarchal control. In "The Story Hearer," Paley's recurrent character Faith goes farther than Selena, objecting to a similar title and explaining exactly what is wrong with such names for women:

At this point the butcher said, what'll you have, young lady?
I refused to tell him.
Jack, to whom, if you remember, I was telling this daylong story, muttered, Oh God, no! You didn't do that again.
I did, I said. It's an insult. You do not say to a woman of my age who looks my age, what'll you have, young lady? I did not answer him. If you say that to someone like me, it really means, What do you want you pathetic old hag?
Are you getting like that now too? he asked.
Look, Jack, I said, face facts. Let's say the butcher meant no harm. Eddie, he's not so bad. He spends two hours commuting to New York from Jersey. Then he spends two hours going back. I'm sorry for his long journey. But I still mean it. He mustn't say it any more.
Eddie, I said, don't talk like that or I won't tell you what I want. (136)

Faith wins her point after a fashion. The butcher does not call her "young lady." His response, however, reveals his inability or unwillingness to find any real alternative to denigrating names for women: "whatever you say, Honey, but what'll you have?" Language change is both important enough to struggle for and exceedingly difficult to implement.

Faith's success with the butcher is mixed, at best. But her protest and her lengthy and lucid explanation of the problem to Jack make it abundantly clear that she knows exactly what is wrong with naming a woman of her age "young lady." Jack's strategy for silencing such protest is to place Faith in a group with other women who are "like that"—i.e., crazy, difficult, strident, unreasonable. Women who make explicit the language bias against women learn that the price of such protest is classification as members of an undesirable group. Jack's remark is an example of the kinds of pressures exerted against women who attempt to break down muteness, but it does nothing to dissuade Faith from voicing her critique.

To correct inaccurate names reveals an underlying belief that such names matter. In the same story, Faith corrects an old friend:

> You don't understand Artaud, he said. I believe that the theatre is the handmaiden of the revolution.
>
> The valet, you mean.
>
> He deferred to my correction by nodding his head. He accepts criticism gracefully, since he can always meet it with a smiling bumper of iron opinion. (136)

Faith objects here to a metaphor that places the female in the subservient position. Her friend could convey his idea as easily with a metaphor of male subordination. She believes it is important to make these corrections, even though the old friend's "smiling bumper of iron opinion" shows that real change is as unlikely here as in the exchange with the butcher.

Some words are used to apply to only one sex, even when the same behavior can be observed in persons of either sex: "Jack . . . unbuttoned his shirt. My face is very fond of the gray-brown hairs of his chest. . . . He began to get a very rosy look about him, which is a nice thing to happen to a man's face. It's not called blushing. Blushing is an expression of shyness and female excitement at the same time. In men it's observed as an energetic act the blood takes on its determined own" ("Listening," 205–206). Although Jack is, in fact, blushing, dominant meanings dictate that men do not blush, so the narrator offers this tongue-in-cheek explanation of the difference. The technique she uses in this passage is a favorite of Paley's. By explaining in simple and patient terms the implicit notions on which dominant usage rests, she exposes the absurdity of dominant categories. Her (only apparently) guileless statement of the enthymeme immediately exposes its illogic to the reader.

In "The Story Hearer," Faith experiences the difficulty of trying to get women's meanings into the record. The butcher announces:

> . . . when I was a boy, a kid—what we called City College—you know it was C.C.N.Y. then, well, we called it Circumcised Citizens of New York.
> Really, said Jim. He looked at me. Did I object? Was I offended?
> The fact of male circumcision doesn't insult me, I said. However, I understand that the clipping of clitorises of young girls continues in Morocco to this day.
> Jim has a shy side. He took his pork butt and said goodbye. (137)

The butcher's joke is, of course, based on an assumption that all City College students are Jewish males. Thus the comment is at once anti-Semitic and sexist. The anti-Semitism is the basis of the joke, while the sexism results from ignoring the presence of women. The muted condition of women is maintained through just such an assumption of males as the normative humans. Faith attempts to shift the conversation to a consideration of women's experience (and thus highlight the male-dominant perspective on which the joke is based) by making a transition from circumcision to clitoridectomy. But her effort is met with awkward silence. The men are embarrassed not by their own omission of women, but because Faith has violated a cultural rule that denies the very existence of clitoridectomy (and even of clitorises, for that matter).

Women who try to tell the truth about women's lives find that the dominant culture can employ a whole range of strategies to silence them or divert them from their point:

> Ruth was still certain that the bad politics and free life of Jiang Qing
> would be used for at least a generation to punish ALL Chinese women.
>   But isn't that true everywhere, said Faith. If you say a simple
> thing like, "There are only eight women in congress," or if you say
> the word "patriarchy," someone always says, Yeah? look at Margaret
> Thatcher, or look at Golda Meir. ("The Expensive Moment," 189)

Faith identifies a familiar patriarchal strategy: justifying the continuation of male dominance by pointing to the failure of token
women to provide an alternative. Meanwhile, the colossal failures of
patriarchy—war, ecological destruction, world hunger—go un-
mentioned.

Faith realizes that dominant beliefs about the lives of women
make it so difficult for woman-centered stories to get a hearing that
sometimes it is better not to try to tell them. In "Listening," Jack,
Faith's companion, asks her to tell him stories about women:

> . . . all those stories are about men, he said. You know I'm more
> interested in women. Why don't you tell me stories told by women
> about women?
>   Those are too private.
>   Why don't you tell them to me? he asked sadly. Well, Jack, you
> have your own woman stories. You know, your falling-in-love
> stories, your French-woman-during-the-Korean-War stories, your
> magnificent-woman stories, your beautiful-new-young-wife stories,
> your political-comrade-though-extremely-beautiful stories . . .
>   Silence—the space that follows unkindness in which little truths
> growl. (203)

Faith refuses to tell Jack the "stories told by women about women"
because "those are too private." She implies that the stories told by
women about women can only be told *to* women. As Faith lists Jack's
"woman stories," she reminds us of the narrow and distorting formulae within which women appear in dominant narratives. The
women in Jack's stories are seen through a romantic and objectifying
lens that is so powerful that it would profane and distort his hearing
of the woman-centered stories Faith could tell.

In "Ruthy and Edie," Faith offers further evidence that stories
structure meaning and that the stories of a dominant tradition often
fail to account for the experiences of female readers. Two small girls

talk "about the real world of boys" (115). Ruthy maintains that one of the advantages of being a boy is that "you could be a soldier." We learn that "Ruthy was a big reader and most interesting reading was about bravery—for instance Roland's Horn at Roncevaux. Her father had been brave and there was often a lot of discussion about this at suppertime. In fact, he sometimes modestly said, Yes, I suppose I was brave in those days. And so was your mother, he added. Then Ruthy's mother put his boiled egg in front of him where he could see it" (116). This passage is revealing both because it shows how Ruthy has identified with the male protagonists in her childhood reading, concluding that theirs are the interesting lives (an experience all too common for young female readers), and because it offers an ironic contrast between the family belief in the father's past bravery and the reality of his present life in which his wife waits on him as if he were helpless.

In "Zagrowsky Tells," Paley herself provides a good explanation for the prevalence of explicit critiques in language in her recent stories. We learn from the narrator Zagrowsky that he is another in the apparently long list of men whose language Faith has corrected: "She got more to say. She also doesn't like how I talk to women. She says I called Mrs. Z. a grizzly bear a few times. It's my wife, no? That I was winking and blinking at the girls, a few pinches. A lie . . . maybe I patted, but I never pinched. Besides, I know for a fact a couple of them loved it. She says, No. None of them liked it. Not one. They only put up with it because it wasn't time yet in history to holler" (165). As women have become conscious of our position as an oppressed group, it has become "time . . . in history to holler"; thus, the women in Paley's most recent fiction register complaints when the language is used against them.

These passages clearly demonstrate Paley's consciousness of the language problems women face when trying to articulate our experience through dominant modes. In a statement from "The Story Hearer" that served as the epigraph for this chapter, Faith provides a good summary of the extent of the problem and the urgency of the situation: "In fact, I am stuck here among my own ripples and tides. Don't you wish you could rise powerfully above your time and name? I'm sure we all try, but here we are, always slipping and falling down into them, speaking their narrow language, though the subject, which is how to save the world—and quickly—is immense" (140).

2
Illuminating the Dark Lives of Women

GP: *Stories illuminate. That's the purpose of a
story for me. To shine a light on what's
dark and give it light. And the balance is
something else . . . It's justice.*
KH: *What are you most interested in
balancing?*
GP: *The dark lives of women.*

—KATHLEEN HULLEY, "INTERVIEW
WITH GRACE PALEY"[1]

Paley's task is to write strongly about women's
lives. To do so requires a strongly woman-
centered language and that, of course, is pre-
cisely what we do not yet have. Consequently Paley, like any woman
who chooses a similar project, must find ways to wrest woman-
centered meanings from the male-dominated language we have
inherited.

The fantasy, of course, is that we could simply jettison the language that distorts or denies women's experiences and start afresh.
But in reality, language change is a process that requires women to
employ the very language that we resist. The problem is how to find
the gaps or fissures through which women can begin to re-present
our absent selves.

Such a venture is possible because language does not exist in a
simple one-to-one correlation with the ideas it communicates. If
such simple correlationships existed, miscommunication would be
impossible, and interpretation would be unnecessary. Language, as
Ferdinand de Saussure has argued, exists in a web of relationship to
and difference from other language, and these interrelationships determine the meaning and value of a given term: "The content of a
word is determined in the final analysis not by what it contains but
by what exists outside it. . . . In a given language, all the words
which express neighboring ideas help define one another's meaning."[2] Consequently, even in the process of inscribing new meanings, a text inscribes such meanings against a backdrop of preexisting
concepts. Jacques Derrida explains:

It is not a question of junking these concepts, nor do we have the
means to do so. Doubtless it is more necessary, from within semi-
ology, to transform concepts, to displace them, to turn them against
their presuppositions, to reinscribe them in other chains, and little
by little to modify the terrain of our work and thereby produce new
configurations; I do not believe in decisive ruptures, in an unequivo-
cal "epistemological break," as it is called today. Breaks are always,
and fatally, reinscribed in an old cloth that must continually, inter-
minably be undone. This interminability is not an accident or con-
tingency; it is essential, systematic, and theoretical. And this in no
way minimizes the necessity and relative importance of certain
breaks, of the appearance and definition of new structures.[3]

Mikhail Bakhtin's concept of dialogism provides a useful framework
for conceptualizing this relationship between any particular utterance and the language that has preceded it: "The living utterance,
having taken meaning and shape at a particular moment in a socially
specific environment, cannot fail to brush up against thousands of
living dialogic threads, woven by socio-ideological consciousness
around the given object of an utterance; it cannot fail to become an
active participant in social dialogue. After all, the utterance arises out
of this dialogue as a continuation of it and as a rejoinder to it—it
does not approach the object from the sidelines."[4]

This description of how language exists in a dialogic relationship
with previous utterances is true of all language, not just language
about women or women's perspectives. But the obstacles for a woman
who would articulate a woman-centered perspective go further. For
dominant texts have defined women not as authors of perception but
as objects of the male gaze. Women are what Margaret Homans has
called "the silent object in the traditional male view of language."[5]
Luce Irigaray sees the denial of female subjectivity as essential to
male discourse. Toril Moi offers this summary of her position:

If one imagined that the woman imagines anything at all, the object
(of speculation) would lose its stability and thus unsettle the subject
itself. If the woman cannot represent the ground, the earth, the inert
or opaque matter to be appropriated or repressed, how can the subject be secure in its status as a subject? Without such a non-subjective
foundation, Irigaray argues, the subject would not be able to con-

struct itself at all. The blindspot of the master thinker's discourse is always woman: exiled from representation, she constitutes the ground on which the theorist erects his specular constructs, but she is therefore also always the point on which his erections subside.[6]

The system Irigaray describes, wherein women can be seen but cannot see, is a system struggling to maintain monologic representation. Dale M. Bauer argues that male monologism is an attempt to drown out other voices; it is destructive of interaction. Yet monologism contains the seeds of its undoing: "no monologic voice, no individual representation of truth . . . can encompass reality."[7] When women refuse to be silent bearers of meaning and emerge as speaking subjects, dominant language, with its denials and distortions of women's experience, becomes problematic.[8]

This chapter examines Paley's semantic strategies for unsettling the denials and distortions of dominant language. These denials and distortions can be grouped into four categories: androcentric language, partial language, exclusionist language, and absolute denials. *A Feminist Dictionary* defines *androcentrism* as male-centeredness. Paley's response to androcentrism, in the largest sense of the word, is the topic of this book. But for the purposes of this chapter, androcentric language refers specifically to language that defines males as the appropriate focus of female attention and language that naturalizes such attention. A common example of such a distortion is the question women who are out together in public regularly encounter, "Are you girls (sometimes "ladies") alone?" According to the terms of androcentric language, women are either with a man or in search of one. Much of the language of romantic thralldom is similarly androcentric. Indeed, all language that defines the male sphere as significant and trivializes the female sphere falls into this category.

A second category of denials and distortions is partial language. In this case, language which describes a part is used as if it described the whole. When this happens the relationship is that of synecdoche, and the result is to obscure or misrepresent the unnamed parts. A particularly common and offensive example of this category of naming is the use of the name *cunt* for "woman." The naming of childbirth and motherhood in the dominant language provides another example: the joy, pleasure, and close bonding that form one part of these experiences are used to name the whole experience, while such aspects as pain, exhaustion, ambivalence, and frustration are omitted from dominant descriptions. Indeed, in this case, the partial names for childbirth and early motherhood are so rigorously enforced that contradictory responses are named as a malady: "postpartum depression." As Sara Maitland notes, "If we are failing to enjoy it, it is easier to say we are poor sick things and some nice drugs will make us feel better, than face up to the fact that mothering is an impossible and treacherous job in our society."[9] Daly seems to have just this sort of denial and distortion in mind when she notes: "Women are now realizing that the universal imposing of names by men has been false because partial. That is, inadequate words have been taken as adequate."[10]

In addition to androcentric and partial language, Paley counters language which is exclusionist. Exclusionist language assumes that the male is universal or paradigmatic (this is obviously a close cousin to androcentric language) and that females belong either wholly outside the category or as a rare exception to the male norm. Most of the professions have been given exclusionist names, so that it can somehow make sense for us to talk about a woman writer or a woman doctor, for instance, while it sounds redundant to speak of a man writer or a man doctor.

Finally, dominant language leaves whole areas of women's experience and perspective unnamed. Here, in the category of absolute denials, we find everything that falls outside of male experience. These are the gaps where women's language ought to be. As Monique Wittig puts it, "The language you speak is made up of signs that rightly speaking designate what men have appropriated. Whatever they have not laid hands on, whatever they have not pounced on like many-eyed birds of prey, does not appear in the language you speak."[11] Of course, as soon as something has a name, it ceases to belong to this category, so examples present a problem. But it is easy to think of words that have entered the language only at the instigation and with the continued pressure of feminists: *sexism, sexual harassment, battered women, displaced homemakers.*[12]

While these seem to be the four major categories of language denials and distortions to which Paley responds, it will become clear as we begin to apply them to her work that they are not necessarily discrete categories. For instance, partial language not only takes a part for the whole, it may also cover a gap in the language, a place where women's experience or perspective is unnamed. Paley's solution, naming the partially named more wholly, will call attention to both categories of denial and distortion. And although androcentric language as construed here specifically focuses female attention on males, in a larger sense all of these denials and distortions evidence androcentrism. Consequently, even though I group Paley's semantic innovations in the following discussion according to these four categories, the examples I draw from her work will show an unruly female tendency to resist reduction into a single category. What the grouping of her responses to these types of language denials and distortions can offer, however, is a structure for examining the various ways in which Paley's semantic innovations amend, replace, contradict, and ultimately transform dominant language.

Paley's primary strategy for unsettling male dominance in language is the sort of "defamiliarization" Victor Shklovskij identifies as crucial to the function of art.[13] One of the maneuvers of defamiliarization is "'rotation' of an object in semantic space (like 'turning a log on a fire'), the shifting of the object out of its typical association into radically different ones, thus presenting a fresh and uneffaced side in a sort of textual space for our perception."[14] What distinguishes Paley's practice of defamiliarization from the maneuver common to all art is that she rotates objects out of masculinist semantic space and into a woman-centered semantic space. The result is somewhat more radical than merely seeing a familiar object afresh—the result is vision transformed.

Androcentric Language

Paley responds to androcentric language through her short stories in a variety of ways. In one of her earliest stories, "Goodbye and Good Luck," the androcentric language is explicitly presented and explicitly responded to in the text. Rosie receives a proposal from one of her suitors to come to Israel for "a big new free happy unusual life." Ruben promises: "'. . . we will raise up the sands of Palestine to make a nation. That is the land of tomorrow for us Jews.' 'Ha-ha, Ruben, I'll go tomorrow then.' 'Rosie!' says Ruben. 'We need strong women like you, mothers and farmers.' 'You don't fool me, Ruben, what you need is dray horses. But for that you need more money.' 'I don't like your attitude, Rose.' 'In that case, go and multiply.

Goodbye'" (*DM*, 16). Ruben cannot imagine a more wonderful future for Rosie than to serve his needs and, by a wonderful coincidence, those of the state. For a woman less attuned to the manipulations of androcentric language, his proposal might be persuasive, for he seems to offer an enlarged role for women when he expresses the need for strong women. But the modifying phrase, "mothers and farmers," makes clear the androcentric bias in his definition of female strength. As usual, when strong free women are spoken of in the dominant language, the goal is not powerful autonomous women, but the harnessing of female energy and independence in the service of males and male institutions. This is an excellent example of what Mary Daly identifies as a reversal, and Paley's text offers a powerful critique of this maneuver. Rosie renames Ruben's "strong women" beasts of burden. Having first redefined Ruben's offer in her own clear and woman-centered terms, she has no difficulty saying no.

The thirteen-year-old narrator of "A Woman, Young and Old" provides another critique of androcentric language, this time with typical Paley irony. The language of romantic thralldom has proved a major strategy for centering the energy and attention of women on the lives and concerns of men. Josephine's mother makes the pursuit of such a romantic attachment a major focus of her life. While describing the father who abandoned her family, Josephine notes that her mother and father "were deeply and irrevocably in love till Joanna and I revoked everything for them" (*DM*, 26). In the primary clause of the sentence, Josephine makes reference to the dominant label of deep and irrevocable love, only to expose in a dependent clause the fabrication involved in a powerful romance ideology which celebrates the permanence of true love and the exclusive claims of romantic thralldom. As the thirteen-going-on-thirty-year-old Josephine reminds us, irrevocable love often becomes all too revocable when the demands of daily life and family intervene.

In "Distance," Paley takes on the dominant definition of women as creatures who have difficulty keeping up with the sexual appetites of males. Mrs. Raftery, one of Faith's neighbors, provides an interesting description of the nightly routine she and her husband followed for years:

> 7:45 p.m. sharp, if there was no company present and the boy out visiting, he liked his pussy. Quick and very neat. By 8:15 he had

showered every bit of it away. I give him his little whiskey. He tried that blabbermouth *Journal-American* for news of the world. It was too much. Good night, Mr. Raftery, my pal.

Leaving me, thank goodness, the cream of the TV and a cup of sweet wine till midnight. Though I liked the attentions as a man he daily give me as a woman, it hardly seemed to tire me as it exhausted him. (*EC*, 19)

In this comic passage, Mrs. Raftery seems at first to play into the dominant stereotype of sexually interested males and disinterested females. But the final sentence in this passage provides an interesting twist, as Mrs. Raftery acknowledges her enjoyment of her husband's attentions and simultaneously gives the lie to the notion that *men* are the inexhaustible sexual partners. Once again, Paley exposes one of the reversals of androcentric language. Of course, for Mrs. Raftery, her husband's lack of energy is not a problem, since she enjoys the opportunity to savor "the cream of the TV" in solitude. Yet her description of the very brief "attentions" her husband devotes to her each evening (thirty minutes from first kiss—if there is time for a kiss—to the end of a shower?) contains an implicit suggestion that the dominant definitions of men as sexually inexhaustible and women as sexually disinterested might also have something to do with the quality of the sex.

In the final story of Paley's second volume, "The Long-Distance Runner," Faith returns to the apartment of her childhood, now located in an African American ghetto. Here she and Mrs. Luddy compare notes across cultures to identify androcentric language. In doing so, they model one of the most powerful tools women have for breaking out of patriarchal meanings into our own language— that is, they talk to each other:

. . . my mother had set beautiful cushions everywhere, on beds and chairs. It was the way she expressed herself, artistically, to embroider at night or take strips of flowered cotton and sew them across ordinary white or blue muslin in the most delicate designs, the way women have always used materials that live and die in hunks and tatters to say: This is my place.

Mrs. Luddy said, Uh huh!

Of course, I said, men don't have that outlet. That's how come they run around so much.

Till they drunk enough to lay down, she said.

Yes, I said, on a large scale you can see it in the world. First they make something, then they murder it. Then they write a book about how interesting it is. (*EC*, 189)

Although this passage does not provide explicit examples of androcentric language, the language of the women exists in a dialogic relationship to such androcentrism. By naming needlework as art and women as creators of art, Faith and Mrs. Luddy challenge the dominant definition of such activity as trivial busywork. But Faith goes farther than that to identify men as the group who lacks a creative outlet and thus behaves in destructive and crazy ways. Male creativity expresses itself in a severely limited way—through analysis of the destruction they have wrought. In this redefinition, Faith and Mrs. Luddy have exposed yet another reversal.

Mrs. Luddy adds to this analysis by describing how white women have participated in the construction and maintenance of androcentric language. She explains that men have been one of her "special pleasures for hard times," but "they turned rotten, white women ruined the best, give them the idea their dicks made of solid gold." Here Mrs. Luddy simultaneously indicts the white racism that objectifies African Americans as sex objects and the collusion of women in the maintenance of male tunnel vision. Faith agrees that "White or black, . . . [men] did think they were bringing a rare gift, whereas it was just sex, which is common like bread, though essential." Again the androcentric depiction of sex as a special male province and the sexual performance of males as phenomenal is exposed. Mrs. Luddy takes the exposure of such androcentric bias one step farther: "Oh, you can do without, she said. There's folks does without" (*EC*, 192). Mrs. Luddy's reminder that "you can do without" resonates throughout Paley's fiction, where men no longer occupy center stage but exist instead in a variety of supporting roles as fathers, husbands, exhusbands, lovers, sons, grocers, pharmacists, and friends.

In her most recent work, Paley continues her project of providing correctives to androcentric language. Lavinia's mother offers this meditation on the relative importance of male and female roles:

My opinion: What men got to do on earth don't take more time
than sneezing. Now a woman walk away from a man, she just know
she loaded down in her body nine months. She got that responsibility on her soul forever.

A man restless all the time owing it to nature to scramble for
opportunity. His time took up with nonsense, you know his conversation got to suffer. A man can't talk. That little minute in his mind
most the time. Once a while busywork, machinery, cars, guns.
("Lavinia: An Old Story," *LD,* 63)

This statement reverses the dominant notion that women's time is
"took up with nonsense" resulting in serious conversational deficiencies. Here the concerns of men are seen as being primarily sexual
("that little minute") with the remaining attention going to "busywork, machinery, cars, guns." Busywork becomes the catchall term
that presumably includes such public occupations as business and
politics. Women, "loaded down in [their bodies] nine months," are
the ones with the serious responsibility.

Paley's responses to androcentric language exist in a dialogic relationship with that language. Often the androcentric language is not
explicitly present in the text, and yet our sense that her language is
innovative derives precisely from the reframing of dominant perspectives. One Paley character announces that "madmen intend to de-
stroy this beautifully made planet" ("Anxiety," *LD,* 101) and with
this statement she redefines foreign policy and politics so as to expose the limited nature of the dominant definitions. The same character describes "the airy scary dreams of scientists and the bulky
dreams of automakers" (103) and in so doing asks us to move away
from the dominant frame that identifies all science and technology as
"progress."

Paley challenges androcentric language throughout her three volumes of short stories. At times (as with the Rosie/Ruben example),
the dominant perspective is articulated by a male speaker; in other
cases a female speaker summarizes the dominant perspective ("they
did think they were bringing a rare gift"), while in many instances
the dominant view is implicit in a dialogic relationship with the
woman-centered perspective articulated in the text ("his time took
up with nonsense, you know his conversation got to suffer"). But in

each case the strong articulation of a female perspective reveals the androcentrism that permeates dominant language.

Exclusionist Language

Paley's earliest work contains no clear examples of the appropriation of exclusionist language for woman-centered purposes. Indeed, four of the five examples discussed in this section come from her most recent volume. This leads to the conclusion that the feminist critique of language developed in the seventies and eighties has strongly influenced Paley's consciousness of and resistance to exclusionist language.

Paley's earliest response to exclusionist language appears in her second volume, *Enormous Changes at the Last Minute.* According to dominant definitions, co-workers, colleagues, and craftsmen have almost always been men and they have most assuredly worked in the public sphere. But in "Faith in a Tree," Paley places these words in a context that provides a powerful challenge to their exclusionist connotations. Faith surveys the other mothers present at the playground. She sees "Kitty, a coworker in the mother trade—a topnotch craftsman. . . . Another colleague, Anne Kraat, is close by on a hard park bench, gloomy, beautiful, waiting for her luck to change" (*EC,* 78). By naming these women co-workers, craftsmen, and colleagues, Faith gives a dignity to the job of motherhood that dominant cultural meanings have denied it and emphasizes the bonds that mothers (often viewed as working in isolation) form with each other. Suddenly, we can see what these women are doing as real work, performed in a context of collaboration with a community of workers. Paley's use of these terms provides a two-edged challenge to dominant meanings: in one direction, Paley has carved out a larger and more powerful self-definition for mothers; in the other direction she has carved out a space for definitions of co-workers, craftsmen, and colleagues that includes not only women but also traditional women's work.

Paley continues her challenge to exclusionist language in *Later the Same Day.* An older Faith remembers babies as "those round, staring, day-in day-out companions of her youth" ("The Expensive Moment," *LD,* 190). "Companions" is an unusual name for babies and elevates them to the status of peers. The unexpectedness of this word in this context directs our attention to the dominant assumption that babies are cute, cuddly possessions or appendages rather than full-fledged persons worthy of respect.

Exclusionist language results whenever gender role definitions assign certain human qualities as the distinctive property of one sex or the other. According to this scheme, strength and the power to protect are, of course, male attributes. But when a middle-aged Faith hears her companion cry out in terror from a nightmare, her description of her response challenges such exclusionist language: "That's O.K. kid, I said, you're not the only one. Everybody's mortal. I leaned all my softening strength against his skinny back" ("The Story Hearer," *LD,* 143). Much has been made of men's role as protector of women; this depiction of woman as the protector of man provides an important corrective. Further, Paley is here expanding our definition of strength to include comfort and nurturance, and suggesting that strength may be "softening" rather than tough—or perhaps "softening" *and* tough. In such an enlargement of the concept of strength, Paley challenges partial language along with exclusionist language.

In a similar maneuver, Paley describes the women in Faith's P.T.A. as "the soft-speaking tough souls of anarchy" ("Friends," *LD,* 77). Here toughness is not only attributed to women but it is further redefined as capable of including a quality usually defined in opposition to toughness—soft speaking. Both these examples suggest that putting women into the definition does not merely alter who can be named with a term—the definition of the term or quality must itself change. In other words, Paley's examples argue that it is not enough to include women in the group of people who can be strong and tough. Woman-centered definitions of strength and toughness will themselves have to change to include such properties of female strength as softness or soft-spokenness.

The last example of exclusionist language is somewhat less obvious than the preceding examples, but Paley clarifies her explication of it by contrast with a dominant model. The subject is the commitment of female friends: "I remember Ann's eyes and the hat she wore the day we first looked at each other. Our babies had just stepped howling out of the sandbox on their new walking legs. We picked them up. I think a bond was sealed then, at least as useful as the vow we'd all sworn with husbands to whom we're no longer married" ("Friends," *LD*, 89). According to dominant definitions, bonds and vows have substance and importance when they occur between men or in marriage between men and women. The bond of female friendship is likely to be ignored or discounted. But in this passage Paley wants it understood that this is an important vow. By contrasting the bond between women friends and the marriage vow, she contrasts women's valuing of commitments between women (in some cases the more lasting and useful commitments) with dominant valuing of the commitments women make to men (also useful, but to whom?).

Partial Language

Unlike the more blatant distortions of androcentric language and the obvious power plays of exclusionist language, partial language simply denies women's experience by failing to tell the whole story. In Paley's most recent collection, Lavinia's mother speaks to the depictions of marriage and motherhood in blissfully romantic terms: "I just as well live out a spinster's peevish time as be consumed by boiling wash water" ("Lavinia: An Old Story," *LD*, 65). If marriage and motherhood were not so shamelessly promoted as happy occupations for all women, viewing them as an endless cycle of boiling wash water would be as partial a view as any other. But within the context of the romanticized definitions promulgated in the dominant language, Paley's image offers an insistently realistic corrective.

In at least one case, Paley's response to partial language takes the form of a comment on the personal, real-life components of abstract concepts. Edie, like so many of Paley's women, grounds her concern for the world in concern for specific children: "Faith was sorry to have mentioned the city in Edie's presence. If you said the word 'city' to Edie, or even the cool adjective 'municipal,' specific children usually sitting at the back of the room appeared before her eyes and refused to answer when she called on them" ("Ruthy and Edie," *LD*, 123). By describing "municipal" as a "cool adjective," Paley exposes the potential of this word to distance us from the personal and human. "Municipal" objectifies; the contrast provided by Edie's compassion reveals the limits of such partial language.

Many of Paley's correctives to partial language serve to provide a more complete and realistic definition of motherhood than that available according to dominant meanings. Although Paley unabashedly celebrates the joys of motherhood, she remains mindful of its costs. Faith's pleasure in her children never omits the hardships of single motherhood: "When I'm not furiously exhausted from my low-level job and that bedraggled soot-slimy house, I praise God for them" ("Faith in a Tree," *EC*, 80).

Paley's fiction even contains the shocking revelation that mothers do not think always and only of their children. When Faith and her friend Ellen are both deathly sick, they have the following conversation:

> "Faith, what'll we do? About the kids. Who'll take care of them? I'm too scared to think."
>
> I was frightened too, but I only wanted the kids to stay out of the bathroom. I didn't worry about them. I worried about me. They were noisy. They came home from school too early. They made a racket. ("Living," *EC*, 61)

Cultural definitions notwithstanding, motherhood is not simply an endless flood of selflessness. Much of the humor in this passage derives from our pleasure in seeing such partial definitions expanded to fit the reality. With this expanded definition, the frame shifts and the problem is located in the limits of dominant definitions rather than in the inability of a particular woman to be superhuman.

Paley also takes on the dominant notion of mothers as omnipotent with respect to their children's development, insisting instead that they do not always know how to raise their children. The children may be "at college or in the hospital or dropouts at home" ("A Conversation with My Father," *EC*, 166), and the equality in that series suggests that one outcome is about as likely as another. Paley has said: "The idea that mothers and fathers raise their kids is ridiculous. . . . You do a little bit—if you're rich, you raise a rich kid, okay—but the outside world is always there, waiting to declare war, to sell drugs, to invade another country, to raise the rents so you can't afford to live someplace—to really color your life." [15]

In "Friends," a story Paley has described as "about grief for the children," [16] Faith notes that "Selena's Abby was not the only one of that beloved generation of our children murdered by cars, lost to war, to drugs, to madness" (*LD*, 72–73). When Faith's son wonders why Selena did not realize her daughter was in trouble, Faith explains: "Listen, Tonto. Basically Abby was O.K. She was. You don't know yet what their times can do to a person" (88). Selena asks Ann about her son Mickey, ". . . a son, a boy of fifteen, who disappears before your very eyes into a darkness or a light behind his own, from which neither hugging nor hitting can bring him" (81). "How did it start?" Selena wants to know. Ann replies: "Nobody knows, nobody knows anything. Why? Where? Everybody has an idea, theories, and writes articles. Nobody knows" (85–86). What all these examples have in common is an awareness that mothers are only one source of influence in their children's lives, a reality that dominant definitions tend to obscure.

Absolute Denials

Although it is important to counter all of the various denials and distortions of male-dominated language, coming to see and to name that for which we have had no language is perhaps most important of all. Much of dominant language denies women's realities in one way or another, but silence is the most profound denial. This project seems to be specifically what Paley has in mind when she speaks of "illuminating what's hidden"[17] or "[shining] a light on what's dark and [giving] it light." The final section of this chapter explores some of the many ways in which Paley's language breaks the silence of patriarchy's absolute denials in order to illuminate "the dark lives of women."

Whenever Paley writes about topics that have been omitted from literature, she is naming the unnamed. Since this enterprise particularly interests Paley, examples of naming the unnamed are abundant in her work. Five topics in particular recur in Paley's development of language for women's experiences: women's focus on men, women's redefinition of men, women and children, female friendship, and the world situation.

Him-itis: Women's Focus on Men

The most clear-cut case of naming the unnamed occurs when one invents a new word, and in one case Paley does exactly that. When

Faith's friend Susan tries to explain another friend's behavior in terms of the friend's involvement with a man, Faith replies, "Susan, you still have him-itis, the dread disease of females" ("Friends," *LD*, 79). Not only does Faith invent a word for this common female condition, she also provides a definition—this is a dread disease. The use of the word *still* in Faith's sentence implies that Susan's case of "him-itis" is a lingering one—she continues to suffer from a malady that ought to have cleared up by now. The creation of this word and its definition direct our attention to a dynamic largely unnamed— the constant focus of female energy and attention on males. Although this is the only instance of Paley actually inventing a word to describe this problem, it is something she has been at work naming for three decades. We saw this earlier when we examined her responses to specifically androcentric language. But she does more than respond to distorting language; she participates in the development of a language that will describe this androcentric focus. In her first volume, a younger Faith asks herself "the sapping question: What is man that woman lies down to adore him?" ("A Subject of Childhood," *DM*, 143). Even raising this question (with its strong echo of Psalm 8) serves to reframe and undermine dominant cultural values.[18] In *Later the Same Day*, Lavinia's mother returns to the problem of him-itis:

> All in every way I look was on their back providing for men or on their knees cleaning up after them.
> I said: Mama, I see you just defile by leaning on every will and whim of Pa's. Now I aim high. To be a teacher and purchase my own grits and not depend on any man. ("Lavinia: An Old Story," *LD*, 65)

In each of these cases, him-itis is not merely named—though calling attention to it is in itself a departure from the silence of the dominant language—it is named as a problem, one that drains female energy and self-care.

Women's Redefinition of Men

Male-authored literary texts have provided us with exhaustive accounts of how men view women, but woman-centered views of men remain largely unavailable in dominant language and literature. Paley has a good bit to say on this subject, and much of what she has to say focuses on men's relationships to their families. In Paley's first collection of stories, Virginia struggles to understand her husband's decision to abandon his family:

> I was happy, but I am now in possession of knowledge that this was wrong. Happiness isn't so bad for a woman. She gets fatter, she gets older, she could lie down, nuzzling a regiment of men and little kids, she could just die of the pleasure. But men are different, they have to own money, or they have to be famous, or everybody on the block has to look up to them from the cellar stairs.
>
> A woman counts her children and acts snotty, like she invented life, but men *must* do well in the world. I know that men are not fooled by being happy. ("An Interest in Life," *DM,* 94)

In this early challenge to male values, the critique is subtle. The materialism of the male perspective is emphasized in the shift from the usual phrase "to have money" to the more possessive construction of "to own money." And although women and men are both described as proud in this passage, the pride of women comes from a belief that they "invented life" while male pride expresses itself in the need to have "everybody on the block . . . look up to them from the cellar stairs"—that is, in a need for dominance and external recognition. Finally, Virginia's conclusion that "men are not fooled by being happy" subtly turns the table, showing just how foolish such a perspective appears when seen through her eyes. Virginia claims to believe that she has been wrong to make happiness and family connection her ultimate values; but the reader is left with the clear sense that her values, with their emphasis on personal connection, are far more sound and solid than the male values of ownership, external recognition, and dominance that she identifies in this passage.

In the same collection, Paley records the ignorance some fathers reveal about their children's lives. The biological and now-absentee father in "The Used-Boy Raisers" visits his ex-wife and children and attempts to assert parental control:

> Faith, he admonished, that boy can't read worth a tinker's damn.
> Seven years old.
>
> Eight years old, I said. ("The Used-Boy Raisers," *DM,* 130)

The absentee father's authority in commenting on his son's education is severely undermined by such ignorance of the facts of his son's life. In Paley's second volume, Phillip shows a similar ignorance about his son:

> Do nine-year-olds talk like that? I think I have a boy who's nine.
> "Yes," said Kitty. "Your Johnny's nine, David's eleven, and Mike's fourteen." ("Faith in a Tree," *EC*, 91–92)

Here the critique of the father's ignorance is even more profound, for the woman who fills in the missing information is not the boys' mother but simply a friend of Phillip's. The implication is that the father has managed to be uncertain of details that even a female friend of the family recalls easily. In the same story, Faith's son expresses a matter-of-fact acceptance of the transient nature of men. Anna attributes her daughter's behavior to her loss of fathers: "'She's lost two fathers,' said Anna, 'within three years.' Tonto stood up to scratch his belly and back, which were itchy with wet grass. 'Mostly nobody has fathers, Anna,' he said" ("Faith in a Tree," *EC*, 95). In each of these passages, male distance or absence from the family is articulated from a female perspective, and the result is not particularly flattering to males.

Paley's naming of male transience continues in her most recent work. Here the woman's perspective is articulated with both more confidence in her own interpretation and more ironic humor than in earlier attempts to name this behavior. Faith prepares to tell Jack the story of her day:

> I said, Shall we begin at the beginning?
> Yes, he said, I've always loved beginnings.
> Men do, I replied. No one knows if they will ever get over this.
> Hundreds of thousands of words have been written, some freelance and some commissioned. Still, no one knows. ("The Story Hearer," *LD*, 133)

Philosophy since Plato has been a search for origins, the beginning, the source of all phenomena. In *Beginnings*, Edward Said reveals the enormous power of the idea of beginnings in Western culture. "Beginning," Said notes, "*authorizes;* it constitutes an authorization for what follows." [19] Luce Irigaray has demonstrated how this search for beginnings dominates patriarchal thought. Indeed, through a particularly peculiar reversal, patriarchal philosophy has developed stories of origins in which males are the point of origin—stories that Irigaray identifies as justifying notions of the male as author, authority, and determiner of what is real. [20] In contrast, women, whose role as childbearers might logically suggest an important connection with beginnings, are left with the responsibility for "middles." This idea seems to be at the core of Adrienne Rich's "Natural Resources." She describes women's performance of the repetitive daily tasks which maintain family and ordinary life and then, in a maneuver that, like the Paley passage, subverts the traditional emphasis on beginnings, concludes:

> I have to cast my lot with those
> who age after age, perversely,
>
> with no extraordinary power,
> reconstitute the world. [21]

Faith's implication that Jack's love of beginnings is part of a general male weakness receives confirmation in a later story, when we learn that he has left her: "Jack had gone off to Arizona for a year to clear his lungs and sinuses and also to have, hopefully, one last love affair, the kind that's full of terrific longing, ineluctable attraction, and so forth. I don't mean to mock it, but it's only natural to have some kind of reaction. Lots of luck, Jack, I said, but don't come home grouchy" ("Listening," *LD,* 209). By ironically describing Jack's behavior from the dominant perspective, Faith clearly articulates the inadequacy of such male meanings to encompass her own perspective on this turn of events. Her ironic tone also reveals her own disdain for this behavior and her refusal to take it seriously. She has now moved to a considerably more powerful position than Virginia's early one in "An Interest in Life."

Women and Children
Children have not held a particularly prominent place in the pages of literature, no doubt reflecting the place they have held in the lives of men. By writing fiction that includes children and harried mothers,

Paley takes an important step in the elimination of women's muted condition:

> *Lidoff:* One special kind of people who appear in your fiction a lot is children.
>
> *Paley:* Yes. See, that interested me a lot. Women and children, and how little they're really used. You also write about things that you haven't read, things that you want to read yourself. And I happen to be very taken with kids.
>
> *Lidoff:* And you don't find much about them in literature?
>
> *Paley:* Yes, a class of women is written about in which the children are taken off by their nanny. All throughout literature women do have children, but they're taken some place else.[22]

Paley's remarks specify that the virtual omission of children from the pages of literature results from the intersection of classism and sexism. But for the middle-class, working-class, and unemployed mothers of Paley's stories, children predominate. For these mothers there are many years when children define the locus of their attention: "Of course, the child Abby was exactly in my time of knowing and in all my places of paying attention—the park, the school, our street" ("Friends," *LD,* 72–73). Such a passage not only names the mother's time of knowing and places of paying attention, but it contains an implicit reminder that fiction has been dominated by a perspective which routinely excludes women's times of knowing and places of paying attention. This list, "the park, the school, the street," not coincidentally names settings that are prominent throughout Paley's work.

At the end of her life a dying Selena reiterates this belief in the importance of children: "We said, each in her own way, How are you feeling, Selena? She said, O.K., first things first. Let's talk about important things. How's Richard? How's Tonto? How's John? How's Chrissy? How's Judy? How's Mickey?" ("Friends," *LD,* 85). With this litany of the children's names, there is a powerful redefining of the dominant notion of important talk.

Female Friendship

The experience of female friendship has been largely ignored or distorted in the dominant culture and literature. The dominant cultural belief that women have little to say to or offer each other is fiercely satirized in Virginia Woolf's *Orlando:*

> So they would withdraw round the Punch bowl which Orlando made it her business to furnish generously, and many were the fine tales they told and many the amusing observations they made for it cannot be denied that when women get together—but hist—they are always careful to see that the doors are shut and that not a word of it gets into print. All they desire is—but hist again—is that not a man's step on the stair? All they desire, we were about to say when the gentleman took the very words out of our mouths. Women have no desires, says this gentleman, coming into Nell's parlour; only affectations. Without desires (she has served him and he is gone) their conversation cannot be of the slightest interest to anyone. "It is well known," says Mr. S. W., "that when they lack the stimulus of the other sex, women can find nothing to say to each other. When they are alone, they do not talk; they scratch." And since they cannot talk together and scratching cannot continue without interruption and it is well known (Mr. T. R. has proved it) "that women are incapable of any feeling of affection for their own sex and hold each other in the greatest aversion," what can we suppose that women do when they seek out each other's society? [23]

Woolf's passage makes the argument for mutedness with respect to female friendship quite forcefully. Women have been careful to conceal the content of our talk and our relationships and men have been more than willing to fill in the gap with their own conclusions. But Paley breaks this silence to name friendships between women as primary and vital.

Women's friendships have become increasingly prominent in Paley's fiction as the women in her stories have grown older and their children have become adults. Indeed, female friendship has become the focus of several Paley stories in her most recent collection. But from her earliest work, Paley describes women's pattern of turning to each other to talk over and get help with our lives. When Virginia's husband deserts her, Mrs. Raftery gives valuable practical advice: "'If that's the case, tell the Welfare right away,' she said. 'He's a bum, leaving you just before Christmas. Tell the cops,' she said. 'They'll provide the toys for the little kids gladly. And don't forget to let the grocer in on it. He won't be so hard on you expecting payment'" ("An Interest in Life," *DM*, 84). Talking things over with other women is the basis of female friendship as it is presented in these stories; it is through talk that the women connect with each other as they go about their daily lives:

> [Faith] had made reasoned statements in the playground and in the A & P while queued up for the cashier, that odd jobs were a splendid way of making out if you had together agreed on a substandard way of life. For she explained to the ladies in whom she had confided her entire life, how can a man know his children if he is always out working? How true, that is the trouble with children today, replied the ladies, wishing to be her friend, they never see their daddies.
> ("Faith in the Afternoon," *EC*, 35–36)

Faith engages strangers in the details of her personal life, and in so doing she forges connections with these women. Although the focus of the conversation might well be men, the point of such talk is to connect with each other: "I believed she was watching and waiting for a particular man. I wanted to discuss this with her, talk lovingly like sisters. But before I could freely say, Forget about that son of a bitch, he's a pig, I did have to offer a few solid facts about myself, my kids, about fathers, husbands, passers by, evening companions, and the life of my father and mother in this room by this exact afternoon window" ("The Long-Distance Runner," *EC*, 191).

Talking it over with other women not only creates connections between women, it gives meaning to the experiences they discuss. In fact, the inability to talk a relationship over with a friend becomes a reason for its failure. When Ruth asks Faith why she is no longer seeing a man she had been interested in, Faith explains, "I couldn't talk to you about it, so it never got thick enough. I mean warped and woofed" ("The Expensive Moment," *LD*, 190). Such talk is the fiber from which they weave their relationships: "They were as busy as bees in a ladies murmur about life and lives. They worked. They took vital facts from one another and looked as dedicated as a kibbutz" ("Faith in the Afternoon," *EC*, 38). This process of women connecting with each other through personal talk has not formed the stuff of traditional narratives. In describing it, Paley fills in an important gap in the language of female friendship.

In addition to building connections through personal talk and making lived experience more real, women friends provide comfort for one another. In an earlier example we saw Mrs. Raftery comforting the abandoned Virginia with practical advice. When Selena asks Ann about her missing son Mickey, Selena's concern makes it easier for Ann to bear the weight of her own worry: "She wouldn't lean too far into Selena's softness, but listening to Selena speak Mickey's name, she could sit in her chair more easily. . . . She was able to rest her body a little bit" ("Friends," *LD,* 85). The women who have come to visit their dying friend, Selena, are reluctant to leave because "we had a long journey ahead of us and had expected a little more comforting before we set off" (77). When Ruth thinks with worry about her daughter Rachel, she says to Faith, "What's the use, . . . you're always wrong." Faith responds: "It was unusual for her [Ruth] to allow sadness. Faith took her hand and kissed it. She said, Ruthy darling. Ruth leaned across the table to hug her. The soup spoon fell to the floor, mixing barley and sawdust" ("The Expensive Moment," *LD,* 187).

This enduring network of women provides support in dealing with children, men, and the world at large. Despite a dominant definition of women as competitors with each other, Paley's women describe a reality in which women share resources. After Ellen's death, Faith remembers her friend:

> . . . I often long to talk to Ellen, with whom, after all, I have done a
> million things in these scary, private years. We drove the kids up
> every damn rock in Central Park. On Easter Sunday, we pasted white
> doves on blue posters and prayed on Eighth Street for peace. Then
> we were tired and screamed at the kids. The boys were babies. For a
> joke we stapled their snowsuits to our skirts and in a rage of slavery
> every Saturday for weeks we marched across the bridges that connect
> Manhattan to the world. We shared apartments, jobs, and stuck-up
> studs. And then, two weeks before last Christmas, we were dying.
> ("Living," *EC,* 61)

Narrative fiction and film have frequently named males as buddies and companions to one another. Paley's descriptions of female friendship illuminate the reality that women are each other's real friends, buddies, and pals.

The World
The women of Paley's fiction name the globe as a fragile and endangered place, which only immediate action can save. Paley makes it clear that she sees a language dominated by male voices as the source of many of the world's problems:

> The only way I can put it is that war is man-made—I mean, it's *really* made by men. If you listen to the radio or look at TV, you see men talking about their particular game, which is war.
>
>   Just turn on the TV—who's talking about this, who's selling it, who's doing it? Listen to the voices, they're all male voices. It's all men, talking, talking, talking, about what missiles should be retrieved, what missiles should be kept—all that stuff is male conversation.[24]

Asked if the act of women talking to each other serves as "a countervailing force to men talking about what they do," she responds: "It is, it's another conversation—and it's drowned out most of the time, but less and less. Our voices are, if not getting a lot louder, getting so numerous. We're talking to each other more and more."[25]

As women's voices enter into the process of defining the world situation, much that has gone unnamed begins to be identified. Such naming has become increasingly prominent in Paley's more recent fiction. For instance, Faith explains the political activity that occupies her time: "Of course, because of this planet, which is dropping away from us in poisonous disgust, I'm hardly ever home" ("Listening," *LD,* 209). In this personification of the planet, Paley shows the earth shrinking in horror from man-made pollution. In another instance, Faith's son Anthony notes the likelihood that Union Carbide will blow up the world. Faith describes her son's world as a "poor, dense, defenseless thing" with "living and dying fastened to its surface and stuffed into its softer parts" ("Friends," *LD,* 89).

The American emphasis on individualism, with its focus on personal life, can be seen as one of the results of a male-dominated discourse. Individualism offers the illusion of escape from the ills of modern life, but Paley regards such a retreat into individualism as an abdication of responsibility for the world situation:

> "You can't give up. And you can't retreat into personal, personal, personal life, because personal, personal, personal life is *hard:* to live in it without any common feelings for others around you is very disheartening, I would think. Some people just fool themselves, decide they have to make a lot of money and then go out and do it, but I can't feel like that." Her voice is low and passionate. "I think these are very rough times. I'm really sorry for people growing up right now, because they have some cockeyed idea that they can get by with their eyes closed; the cane they're tapping is money, and that won't take them in the right direction." [26]

In "The Story Hearer," Faith expresses a similar concern with the limits of individualism: "I am trying to curb my cultivated individualism, which seemed for years so sweet. It was my own song in my own world and, of course, it may not be useful in the hard time to come" (*LD*, 133). Here, Paley redefines individualism, a cornerstone of American thought, as an ideology that had some merit in the past but that has outlived its usefulness. [27] The "hard time to come" will demand a different structure for our relationship to the world.

Rather than the obsessive concern with self-interest that has come to dominate modern American life, Paley argues persistently that we need to form connections and build community on the basis of common concerns and common causes: "One of the things that really runs through all the stories, because they're about groups of women, is the sense that what we need now is to bond; we need to say 'we' every now and then instead of 'I' every five minutes." [28] For Paley, the global scope of the problems the world faces means that nationalism and individualism are equally anachronistic. But the solution lies in a development of qualities that male dominance has suppressed. She is convinced that the muted female capacity for connection and community offers an antidote to the dangers of individualism.

Paley also perceives children as an important grounding and point of origin for political action. In "Faith in a Tree," her son Richard's powerful reaction to an anti-Vietnam protest has a profound effect on Faith: "And I think that is exactly when events turned me around, changing my hairdo, my job uptown, my style of living and telling. Then I met women and men in different lines of work, whose minds were made up and directed out of that sexy playground by my children's heartfelt brains, I thought more and more and every day about the world" (*EC*, 99–100).

In an interview, Paley has described a similar connection between the common concern of mothers for their children and political action:

> "One of the nice things that happens when you have kids . . . is that you really get involved in the neighborhood institutions. If you don't become a local communitarian worker then, I don't know when you do. For instance, when my kids were very little, the city was trying to push a road through Washington Square Park to serve the real estate interests. We fought that and we won; in fact, having won, my friends and I had a kind of optimism for the next 20 years that we might win something else by luck." She laughs, as amused by her chronic optimism as she is convinced of its necessity. "It took a lot of worry, about the kids and buses going through the park at a terrific rate, to bring us together. You can call it politics or not; it becomes a common concern, and it can't be yours alone any more."[29]

Here politics is specifically defined as originating in a common concern for the welfare of the children.

Such a sensibility permeates Paley's language for the world situation. A daughter is "that little girl whose future is like a film which suddenly cuts to white" and "a little doomed person" ("Anxiety," *LD*, 101). Children are "lovely examples of what may well be the last generation of humankind" ("Anxiety," 102). Naming the children in this way also names a perspective on the world that has the potential to transform both world politics and personal relationships.

Even a birthday celebrated by four old friends becomes an occasion for speaking about a shared concern for the state of the world. Ruthy's birthday wish, made jointly with Ann ("Come on, Ann, we've got to blow this out together. And make a wish. I don't have the wind I used to have"), is "that this world wouldn't end." Ann calls on her friends to "go forth with fear and courage and rage to save the world" ("Ruthy and Edie," *LD*, 124).

Paley names a world in which women share concern for a planet poised on the brink of destruction, a world whose very survival depends on the creation of powerfully woman-centered speech. "The subject, which is how to save the world—and quickly—is immense." Paley, with a firm belief in the transforming power of language, intends nothing less.

3
What Is There to Laugh?

Naturally it was a joke, only what is there to laugh?

—"ZAGROWSKY TELLS," *LD*, 160

P ublicly funny women are rare in our culture. This is not particularly surprising given the widespread cultural beliefs that women lack a sense of humor and that public displays of wit by women in mixed groups are somehow inappropriate. Although changes have begun to occur here as elsewhere, female comedians and female-authored comic strips, for instance, are still relatively unusual.[1]

While women have not created public expressions of humor as frequently as men, we have often been the butt of dominant humor, and the portrait of women that has emerged serves male dominance. As Gloria Kaufman notes in the introduction to an anthology of feminist humor:

> By A.D. 101, in Juvenal's "Sixth Satire," the female stereotype is firmly defined as nasty, lying, vicious, pretentious, emasculating, garrulous, aggressive, vulgar, nymphomaniacal, gluttonous, dishonest, shame-less, greedy, selfish, quarrelsome, impertinent, and disgusting. Notably absent in Juvenal is the idea of woman as stupid and ineffectual. Instead, she is offensively intelligent—the legitimate castrating bitch. When we add stupidity and ineffectuality to the Juvenalian list, we have a fairly complete picture of the stereotypical woman targeted by male humorists.[2]

Women are not likely to generate as much public humor as males, as long as such derogatory depictions of women form a staple of jokes and comic routines. As feminist comedian Kate Clinton explains, "Men have used humor against women for so long—we know implicitly whose butt is the butt of their jokes—that we do not trust humor."[3]

Yet feminists have begun to chart the existence of an alternative female tradition of humor, one that relies less on jokes and set pieces and more on anecdotal and situational humor.[4] More likely to find expression in private than in public settings, this tradition emphasizes connection, compassion, self-disclosure, and reciprocal sharing of perspectives (in contrast to the more hostile put-down tradition of male humor).[5] Mercilee Jenkins links the difference in male and female traditions of humor to differences in conversational style: "Women and men in same-sex groups experience a different kind of 'likeness' due to their status in society and their roles and relationships. Men in their groups seem to be saying, 'I'm great. *I'm great, too*. Gee we're a great bunch of guys.' In contrast, women seem to be saying, 'Did this ever happen to you? *Yeah*. Oh, good, I'm not crazy . . .'"[6] The recognition that the craziness might be in the system rather than in the perspective of an individual woman is the beginning of a radicalizing use of humor. Clinton describes humor with the potential to deconstruct male dominance and subvert the status quo: "Feminist humor is serious, and it is about the changing of this world. It is about making light in this land of reversals, where we are told as we are laughing, tears streaming down our faces, that we have no sense of humor."[7]

Grace Paley is an unabashedly funny woman. Critics have commented consistently on the humor inherent in her innovative use of language ("startling, comic-bizarre language")[8] and her irrepressible urge to "make light" ("a kind of running thread of humor underlying nearly every passage").[9] To be a funny woman in a public forum is already to be a breed apart, but Paley goes farther: she is a funny woman whose humor does not come at the expense of women:

JT: I want to talk about your humor. It's not unusual, even in literature by women, to find that women are the butt of the joke. Society might be seen as wrong to place such impossible demands on women, but women are more wrong for their inability to cope with those demands. Maybe they go crazy or

they can't function as superwomen, so they somehow fail. But
in your work, the women are *fine;* the world is crazy.
GP: Well, it's true, isn't it? (Laughter.) [10]

Such a distinction marks the difference between female humor
and feminist humor. Feminist humor is transformative, locating absurdity in the perpetuation of male dominance.[11] By inviting women
to laugh together at the absurdity of a system that misnames us and
our world, Paley employs humor to disrupt the status quo. "Laughter is the most subversive agent in literature," notes Alicia Ostriker.[12]
This chapter analyzes humor as a key element in Paley's transformation of language and illumination of women's lives.

Humor plays a critical role in Paley's fiction. Not only does Paley
make hilariously inventive use of language, but her characters tell
jokes and crack frequent one-liners. They take their jokes seriously
enough to not only tell them but talk about them. Sometimes their
humor falls flat, and they have to explain that "I was only joking"
("Dreamer in a Dead Language," *LD,* 36). At other times they direct
our attention to their ability to joke despite misfortune: "You see, I
can crack a little joke because look at this pleasure" ("Zagrowsky
Tells," *LD,* 169). Jokes are understood to arise from a particular
world view and have political implications, as Faith's critique of the
political shortcomings of the grocer's C.C.N.Y. joke (see chapter 2)
makes clear.[13]

In "A Conversation with My Father," the narrator's father criti-
cizes her inability to write a story without jokes.[14] He sees this as a
major weakness. "With you it's all a joke," he comments, and then
later, "Jokes . . . As a writer that's your main trouble. You don't want
to recognize it" (*EC,* 163, 166–67). Finally he says sadly, "Jokes. Jokes
again" (167). Like the writer in this story, Paley cannot write stories
without also writing a series of wisecracks, one-liners, and jokes. But
whereas the father in "A Conversation" sees the author's joking as an
indication of her unwillingness to take her writing and her characters
seriously, this study sees Paley's joking as central to her absolutely
serious challenge to dominant meanings.

Wordplay is central to Paley's humor. Paley has commented on the
importance of wordplay in her work: "There's a lot of wordplay.
Partly because there's a lot of play; there has to be play in everybody's
work. There's a lot of play and variety or else it's wrong. Writing that

does not have play in it is often half-dead."[15] The two preceding chapters offer numerous hilarious examples of Paley's considered and innovative approach to language.[16] Her wordplay often occurs in the space between dominant and woman-centered realities. Many of the revised definitions offered in the preceding chapter are funny because they play with the discrepancy between dominant definitions and the experience of women. For instance, naming the other mothers in the playground "co-workers," "craftsmen," and "colleagues" amuses us because the dominant meanings for these words exclude mothers, who, in fact, have never been seen by the dominant culture as doing "real" work. Yet such terms become suddenly apt if we assume a perspective that values the work of women and appreciates the collegiality mothers share with each other. The humor results because such definitions invite us to appreciate our double vision as insiders and outsiders, a part of the dominant culture and yet excluded from it. And the laughter is subversive because we cannot appreciate this juxtaposition without perceiving the absurdity of the dominant meanings and without ceasing to take such false definitions seriously. Any of the areas of redefinition identified in the preceding chapter could also be analyzed as a source and location of humor in Paley's work. Rather than reiterate these insights, however, this chapter seeks the sources of Paley's humor.

One of the most basic characteristics of Paley's humor is her irreverence. She refuses to take seriously any of the sacred cows of male dominance, choosing a stance that Adrienne Rich has named "disloyalty to civilization."[17] Her humor is survivalist humor—that is, humor created in order to survive oppression. Such humor is generated by an oppressed group to call attention to the absurdities and tunnel vision of a dominant perspective that assumes its own universality. Survivalist humor takes place on the margins of the culture in the space between dominant and muted meanings.

Two of the sources of Paley's comic impulse are earthiness and optimism, qualities she shares with other contemporary women writers. Her humor is simultaneously down-to-earth and hopeful.

A third important source of the humor Paley employs to articulate women's experiences is Jewish humor, a major survivalist tradition. As a member of two muted groups, Paley has derived some powerful comic devices from her Jewish heritage and employed them in the service of illuminating women's reality.

Earthiness

Women as defined in the pages of dominant fiction are alternatively mysterious, ethereal, other-worldly creatures or depraved, shameful vessels of corruption. The virgin-whore dichotomy in dominant images of women is too well established to require reiterating here. In Paley's fiction, irreverent humor becomes one of the primary means for challenging such depictions of women. Writing about contemporary women's poetry, Ostriker notes that "among other sorts of 'fracture of order' designed to combat the oppressor's language, earthiness, bawdry, and comedy abound."[18] "Earthy" is an excellent word to apply to Paley's humor, for her humor is "down-to-earth and practical," "of this world," and "hearty and unashamed."[19] In a world that has posited women's bodies and physical natures as a site of shame, this is no mean feat.

The women in Paley's fiction are frankly and heartily sexual beings. Faith becomes pregnant "in happy overindulgence" and learns to love the properties in herself that "extracted such heart-warming activity" from her husband ("Faith in the Afternoon," *EC,* 35). The night is a time for "sleep, sex, and affection" to "take their happy turns" ("Dreamer in a Dead Language," *LD,* 15). Mrs. Raftery notes that she "liked the attentions as a man he daily give me as a woman" ("Distance," *EC,* 19). These women express their pleasure. Lovemaking is a "noisy disturbance" ("Enormous Changes," *EC,* 124) and the occasion of "incessant happy noises" ("A Woman, Young and Old," *DM,* 40). Such phrases probably will not cause the reader to laugh out loud, but their gentle redefinition of women as enthusiastically sexual beings provides a strong undercurrent of comic irreverence.

In Paley's work, women at any age are likely to find themselves thinking and fantasizing about sex. In "A Woman, Young and Old," two sisters talk about their desire for a man, a desire articulated in sexual terms: "Aunty Liz is seventeen and my mother talks to her as though she were totally grown up. Only the other day she told her she was just dying for a man, a real one, and was sick of raising two girls in a world just bristling with goddamn phallic symbols. Lizzy said yes, she knew how it was, time frittered by, and what you needed was a strong kind hand at the hem of your skirt" (*DM,* 25). In the park with her children, Faith (in contrast to the mothers in the dominant tradition, who, of course, lose all sexual feelings on learning they have conceived) has a strong sexual response as she watches Phillip flirt with her friend Anna:

> "Say!" said Phillip, getting absolutely red with excitement, blushing from his earlobes down into his shirt, making me think as I watched the blood descend from his brains that I would like to be the one who was holding his balls very gently, to be exactly present so to speak when all the thumping got there.
>
> Since it was clearly Anna, not I, who would be in that affectionate position, I thought I'd better climb the tree again just for the oxygen or I'd surely suffer the same sudden descent of blood. ("Faith in a Tree," *EC*, 97)

Not only young women, but also women "later-in-life, which has so much history and erotic knowledge but doesn't always use it" ("Listening," *LD*, 206), experience desire. In "Listening," Faith's sons are grown and busy with their own lives and her companion Jack has abandoned her in pursuit of "one last love affair," but none of this has put her beyond the reach of sexual feeling:

> A man in the absolute prime of life crossed the street. For reasons of accumulating loneliness I was stirred by his walk, his barest look at a couple of flirty teenage girls; his nice unimportant clothes seemed to be merely a shelter for the naked male person.
>
> I thought, Oh, man, in the very center of your life, still fitting your skin so nicely, with your arms probably in a soft cotton shirt and the shirt in an old tweed jacket and your cock lying along your thigh in either your right or left pants leg, it's hard to tell which, why have you slipped out of my sentimental and carnal grasp? (209)

If this passage surprises the reader, it does so because the intersection of ageism and sexism in language has left us without such frank depictions of late-middle-age female sexual desire. Although the pages of fiction are replete with descriptions of male longing and male fantasies about women, these scenes from Paley offer a glimpse of previously muted experience. The humor, as with so much of Paley's work, derives from our encounter with a description of experience that the dominant discourse has defined out of existence and that we nevertheless recognize as an apt portrayal of actual lived experience.

The women in Paley's stories make no pretense of sexual inno-
cence. Instead, they seem to enjoy shocking their listeners with their
down-to-earth acknowledgment of sexual reality. When Virginia's
friend John announces "Children come from God," Virginia retorts:
"You're still great on holy subjects aren't you? You know damn well
where children come from." She then informs us that, "He did know.
His red face reddened further" ("An Interest in Life," *DM*, 88). Mrs.
Raftery takes particular delight in earthy reports and advice:

> Ginny's husband ran off with a Puerto Rican girl who shaved
> between the legs. This is common knowledge and well known or I'd
> never say it. When Ginny heard that he was going around with this
> girl, she did it too, hoping to entice him back, but he got nauseated
> by her and that tipped the scales.
>
> Men fall for terrible weirdos in a dumb way more and more as
> they get older; my old man, fond of me as he constantly was, often
> did. I never give it the courtesy of my attention. My advice to moth-
> ers and wives: Do not imitate the dimwit's girl friends. You will be
> damnfool-looking, what with your age and all. Have you heard the
> saying "Old dough won't rise in a new oven"? ("Distance," *EC*, 17)

The earthy irreverence of these women often serves as an antidote
to a false romanticism: "So we slept, his arms around me as sweetly
as after the long day he had probably slept beside his former wife
(and I as well beside my etc. etc. etc.)" ("The Story Hearer," *LD*,
142). At other times humor counters false dominant meanings regarding women's sexual motivation. In a culture that offers "prostitute" as one of the essential definitions for women,[20] Faith responds
with heavy sarcasm to her father's assumption that she is sleeping
with three different men for the money: "Oh sure, they pay me all
right. How'd you guess? They pay me with a couple of hours of their
valuable time. They tell me their troubles and why they're divorced
and separated and they let me make dinner once in a while. They play
ball with the boys in Central Park on Sundays. Oh sure, Pa, I'm paid
up to here" ("Dreamer in a Dead Language," *LD*, 31–32). In another
instance, a Paley character offers a cheerful reversal of the dominant
definition of "moral turpitude." Josephine, describing her mother's
enthusiastic response to a new boyfriend, announces, "Her moral
turpitude took such a lively turn that she gave us money for a

Wassermann" ("A Woman, Young and Old," *DM*, 39). In this cheerful celebration of sexuality, moral turpitude is transformed from "inherent baseness" and "depravity" into the source of generosity and the explanation for the mother's acceptance of Josephine's marriage plans.

Grounded in ordinary daily life, these women derive humor from a practical view of events, an earthiness that extends beyond the sexual. When Virginia's husband announces his plan to abandon his family and join the army, Virginia reports, "I asked him if he could wait and join the Army in a half hour, as I had to get groceries" ("An Interest in Life," *DM*, 81). With four children to care for, Virginia has no choice but to be grounded in the practical. This response to her husband's imminent departure has the effect of taking his desertion less seriously than her need for childcare while she gets groceries. In "The Immigrant Story," Faith demonstrates a similar insistence on the practical. Jack tells Faith that as a boy he found his father sleeping in the crib because his mother "didn't want him to fuck her." Faith replies, "I don't believe it. . . . Unless she's had five babies all in a row or they have to get up at 6 a.m. or they both hate each other, most people like their husbands to do that." When Jack insists that she was trying to make his father feel guilty, Faith notes that "anyone whose head hasn't been fermenting with the compost of ten years of gluttonous analysis" could come up with a more reasonable (practical) explanation. "The reason your father was sleeping in the crib was that you and your sister who usually slept in the crib had scarlet fever and needed the decent beds and more room to sweat, come to a fever crisis, and either get well or die" ("The Immigrant Story," *EC*, 172–173). To Faith, "gluttonous analysis" is the source of complex psychological explanations which obscure the simply practical realities of daily life.

This practical earthiness excludes a falsely romantic depiction of women's physical life. When Rosie asks her lover Vlashkin how a Jewish boy grew up so big, he replies, "My mama nursed me till I was six. I was the only boy in the village to have such health." Rosie's shocked response directs our attention away from his romantic view of breast-feeding to an earthy appreciation of the mother's experience: "My goodness, Vlashkin, six years old? She must have had shredded wheat there, not breasts, poor woman." Vlashkin's reply reveals his difficulty with this earthy resistance to romanticism: "'My mother was beautiful,' he said. 'she had eyes like stars'" ("Goodbye and Good Luck," *DM,* 10). Faith insists similarly on the realities of female physical life in "Living," when she provides a comic yet realistic account of a time when she thought she "was going to bleed forever":

> I could hardly take my mind off this blood. Its hurry to leave me was draining the red out from under my eyelids and the sunburn off my cheeks. It was all rising from my cold toes to find the quickest way out. . . .
> I felt a great gob making its dizzy exit.
> "Can't talk," I said. "I think I'm fainting."
> Around the holly season, I began to dry up. My sister took the kids for a while so I could stay home quietly making hemoglobin, red corpuscles, etc., with no interruption. I was in such first-class shape by New Year's I nearly got knocked up again. (*EC,* 60–61)

This description of menstrual flooding (or possibly hemorrhaging) is funny because of its flip tone ("a great gob") and also because we are surprised to find such a description in the pages of literature. After all, anything associated with menstrual bleeding is not even supposed to be mentioned in mixed company, much less in the public forum of a literary work (unless of course, it results in the death of the heroine).

Paley's earthiness is not an extraordinary feature of women's humor, it is simply a muted feature. In all-female groups in private settings, women have a lively ribald tradition. Nancy Walker, in *A Very Serious Thing: Women's Humor and American Culture,* cites a number of studies that attest to the vitality of earthy humor among all-female groups gathered around the kitchen table, particularly when such groups include postmenopausal women who are freed by virtue of their age from intense social pressure to behave like "ladies."[21]

In Paley's fiction, such female bawdry goes public, with literary characters who refuse to keep quiet about their sexual, physical, and resolutely earthbound selves, thereby functioning as a primary source of subversive humor. In all of these examples, the earthy practicality of Paley's women challenges the falsely romanticized, sanitized, desexualized, or eroticized dominant views of women. The juxtaposition of dominant misrepresentations and actual lived experience produces the laughs, laughs accompanied by a sigh of relief as women readers recognize, "Oh, good, I'm not crazy."

Optimism

Yet another source of Paley's humor is the irrepressible optimism of these works. Ostriker writes about the appearance of such a tone in contemporary women's poetry: "From time to time there surfaces a tone difficult to describe in our ordinary critical discourse: a species of irony, it seems, but vulgar and cheerful in contrast to the resigned and cruel ironies modernism teaches us to scent out as a primary signal of the cultivated author. This peculiar tone may be one of the chief contributions women are making to our literary and personal repertoires." [22] Ostriker describes this tone as one of "giddy glee" and observes that "it is as if instead of the universe revealing itself as irrationally cruel and meaningless, it revealed itself as irrationally (for we are supposed to know better) benign." [23]

Such optimism permeates Paley's fiction and functions as a recurrent comic impulse. One result of this optimism is Paley's resistance to narrative resolution, expressed in the statement that "everyone, real or invented, deserves the open destiny of life" (this resistance to narrative closure is discussed more fully in the next chapter). Paley's stories portray a chronic hopefulness that, despite all manner of human suffering, things may, in the end, turn out happily after all. Such optimism exists not by ignoring "wars, deception, broken homes, all the irremediableness of modern life" ("A Woman, Young and Old," *DM,* 25), but by the "interest in life" that continues in spite of and through such calamities: "In the middle of my third beer, searching in my mind for the next step, I found the decision to go on 'Strike It Rich.' I scrounged some paper and pencil from the toy box and I listed all my troubles, which must be done in order to qualify. The list when complete could have brought tears to the eye of God if He had a minute. At the sight of it my bitterness began to improve. All that is really necessary for survival of the fittest, it seems, is an interest in life, good, bad, or peculiar" ("An Interest in Life," *DM,* 98). In this passage, Virginia is cheered not by self-delusion—she sees the difficulties of her situation quite clearly—but by a recognition that even the bad and peculiar are signs of life.

Like Paley's character Lavinia, many of the people in these stories seem, despite personal difficulties, to have been "born in good cheer" ("Lavinia," *LD,* 64). A group of women friends is "all, even Edie, ideologically, spiritually, and on puritanical principle against despair" ("Ruthy and Edie," *LD,* 122). Their optimism derives from a profound belief in the possibility for change: "Though terrible troubles hang over them, such as the absolute end of the known world quickly by detonation or slowly through the easygoing destruction of natural resources, they are still, even now, optimistic, humorous, and brave. In fact, they intend enormous changes at the last minute" ("Enormous Changes," *EC,* 126). A hard-nosed awareness that our planet is indeed "at the last minute" is nevertheless bearable because, as long as there is a future, there is still the potential for change. Such a perspective eschews the deliberate despair of modernism: "Luckily, I learned recently how to get out of that deep well of melancholy. Anyone can do it. You grab at the roots of the littlest future, sometimes just stubs of conversation. Though some believe you miss a great deal of depth by not sinking down down down" ("Friends," *LD,* 83). Here Paley not only elucidates her own optimistic perspective but mocks the studied melancholy of modernism.

This insistence on seeing plainly the grimmest aspects of modern life while grabbing at "the roots of the littlest future" results in some wildly comic juxtapositions. In "The Long-Distance Runner," Faith comments on New York: "I wanted to stop and admire the long beach. I wanted to stop in order to think admiringly about New York. There aren't many rotting cities so tan and sandy and speckled with citizens at their salty edges" (*EC,* 181). Faith's ability to admire her decaying urban landscape recurs in "The Story Hearer": "The *Times* was folded on the doormat of 1-A. I could see it was black with earthquake, war, and private murder. Clearly death had been successful everywhere but not—I saw when I stepped out the front door—on our own block. Here it was springtime, partly because of the time of the year and partly because we have a self-involved block-centered street association which has lined us with sycamore and enhanced us with mountain ash, two ginkgoes, and here and there, (because we are part of the whole) ailanthus, city saver" (*LD,* 134).

Paley's ability to express such optimism and faith in humanity without ever veering into sentimentality is largely achieved through her wry, knowing, comic voice. Marianne DeKoven illustrates her discussion of this use of the comic to displace potential sentimentality with a Paley description of Mrs. Hegel-Shtein:

> "On deep tracks, the tears rolled down her old cheeks. But she had smiled so peculiarly for seventy-seven years that they suddenly swerved wildly toward her ears and hung like glass from each lobe." The image of Mrs. Hegel-Shtein's tears swerving along deep tracks, formed by seventy-seven years of peculiar smiling, to hang from her ear lobes like crystals, is so striking that it appropriates most of our attention as we read, preventing us from noticing the pathos which we nonetheless feel. The fate of Mrs. Hegel-Shtein's tears is exactly the fate of our own. They fall, but they are "wildly" diverted along literally comic tracks to become something other than tears, something not at all commonplace; in fact, something transcendent: they crystallize into literary epiphany.[24]

Grounded in the demands and pleasures of daily life, Paley's optimism resists the dominant literature's modernist despair, insisting on the validity of a perspective that hopes always for enormous changes for the better. Perhaps modernist despair is one of the luxuries of male dominance, while those who exist on the margins have to believe that the world can change—that oppression must end. Accused of having "a rotten rosy temperament," Faith staunchly defends her optimism: "I believe I see the world as clearly as you do, I said. Rosiness is not a worse windowpane than gloomy gray when viewing the world" ("The Immigrant Story," *EC*, 173, 174). Through the windowpane of Paley's comic optimism, we begin to suspect that the sterility of the modern landscape revealed to us in dominant literature may yet be found, when viewed through the eyes of women, to contain irrepressible signs of life.

Jewish Humor

No discussion of Paley's use of humor to break down mutedness would be complete without a consideration of her use of Jewish humor. Paley herself has talked about the importance of Jewish humor in her work:

GP: When you talk about my humor, a lot of it is related to women and a lot of it is Jewish, plain old Jewish humor from around. Where the Jews make these jokes in which they are presumably the butt. In which they allow themselves that. But they're not. Like the joke Faith's father makes in that story, where he says give me another globe. That's a typical Jewish joke, where the Jew says "well, it's probably my fault, but still, give me another globe."

JT: So in a way, you're using this strategy that Jewish people have developed for making themselves central in a world that defines them as marginal, and transferring it to women.

GP: Well, to some degree. I think you put it in a very clear way. I could never have said it like that. I mean you would think that *all* oppressed people would understand all other oppressed people. However, this is not so. (Laughs.)

JT: It also seems to me that it's your very existence as a member of two marginalized groups, women and Jewish people, that allows you to *see* so much.

GP: Umhmm. And also very verbal people.[25]

These comments contain several suggestions that can help us to understand not only Paley's use of humor but also how she has managed to create a body of work that offers such a powerful challenge to dominant meanings. As a Jewish woman, Paley was born into a doubly muted state. Although the costs of double mutedness are high, such an experience places one so clearly outside access to the dominant patriarchal power structure that it may, in some cases, lead to a more radical critique of dominant meanings. Paley's recurrent character Faith argues that offering a critique of dominance derived from their experience of marginality is what distinguishes Jews (and one might argue by extension, other marginalized groups as well) as the chosen people: "Jews have one hope only—to remain a remnant in the basement of world affairs—no, I mean something else—a splinter in the toe of civilizations, a victim to aggravate the conscience" ("The Used-Boy Raisers," *DM,* 132).

In addition, Paley notes that the Jewish culture she grew up in is an extremely verbal culture and a culture that has learned strategies for coping as a group with centuries of unrelenting oppression. For a verbal people, language will offer a crucial means of resistance, and humor can serve as one of the more subversive strategies available through language. Walker's study of women's humor identifies Jewish people as "the single group that has affected American humor more than any other group. . . . With their long tradition of minority status, the Jewish people developed, centuries before their immigration to the United States, a highly refined humorous tradition that both acknowledges their position as a minority and makes fun of the oppressor."[26]

For Paley, there are some important connections to be made between female and Jewish experiences of subordination. In "Friends," Paley again links the two. Faith's friend Ann, angry because Faith is making jokes in the midst of their troubles, accuses Faith of always having been lucky:

> Well, some bad things have happened in my life, I said.
> What? You were born a woman? Is that it?
> She was, of course, mocking me this time, referring to an old discussion about feminism and Judaism. Actually, on the prism of isms, both of those do have to be looked at together once in a while.
> (*LD,* 81)

Certainly looking at feminism and Judaism together helps to account for Paley's creation of woman-centered humor. In order to consider the connection between Paley's use of Jewish humor and her use of humor to deconstruct women's mutedness, we need to understand how the characters in Paley's works employ humor as a critique of anti-Semitism and the pressures toward assimilation.

The joke that Paley refers to in the interview quoted above appears in "Dreamer in a Dead Language." Faith's father tells it to Faith and her two sons, Richard and Anthony:

> There's an old Jew. He's in Germany. It's maybe '39, '40. He comes around to the tourist office. He looks at the globe. They got a globe there. He says, Listen, I got to get out of here. Where do you suggest, Herr Agent, I should go? The agency man also looks at the globe. The Jewish man says, Hey, how about here? He points to America. Oh, says the agency man, sorry, no, they got finished up with their quota. Ts, says the Jewish man, so how about here? He points to France. Last train left already for there, too bad, too bad.

Nu, then to Russia? Sorry, absolutely nobody they let in there at the present time. A few more places . . . the answer is always, port is closed. They got already too many, we got no boats . . . So finally the poor Jew, he's thinking he can't go anywhere on the globe, also he can't stay where he is, he says oi, he says achi he pushes the globe away, disgusted. But he got hope. He says, So this one is used up, Herr Agent. Listen—you got another one?

Oh, said Faith, what a terrible thing. What's funny about that? I hate that joke.

I get it, I get it, said Richard. Another globe. There is no other globe. Only one globe, Mommy? He had no place to go. On account of that old Hitler. Grandpa, tell it to me again. So I can tell my class. (*LD,* 19–20)

Faith hates this joke because she finds the reality of the holocaust on which it is based too horrible to joke about. Later she explains her response to her sons:

Hey boys, look at the ocean. You know you had a great-grand-father who lived way up north on the Baltic Sea, and you know what, he used to skate, for miles and miles and miles along the shore, with a frozen herring in his pocket.

Tonto couldn't believe such a fact. He fell over backwards into the sand. A frozen herring! He must've been a crazy nut.

Really Ma? said Richard. Did you know him? he asked. No, Richie, I didn't. They say he tried to come. There was no boat. It was too late. That's why I never laugh at that story Grandpa tells.

Why does Grandpa laugh? (35)

Grandpa laughs in celebration of the same irrepressible optimism that permeates Paley's fiction. The Jew of this story is in a seemingly hopeless situation and yet he has hope. In one sense he is the butt of the joke, for his request for another globe is absurd. Yet in another sense he gives testimony to the strength of spirit that has enabled Jewish people to survive through centuries of vicious anti-Semitism. In *The Joys of Yiddish,* Leo Rosten explains that "Humor . . . serves the afflicted as compensation for suffering, a token victory of brain over fear. A Jewish aphorism goes: 'When you're hungry, sing; when you're hurt, laugh.' The barbed joke about the strong, the rich, the heartless powers-that-be is the final citadel in which human pride can live."[27]

This ability to laugh through one's tears, to mock even the most difficult circumstances, is seen throughout Paley's work. In "Zagrowsky Tells," Zagrowsky describes his response to an encounter his wife had with an African American man on the subway:

> In the subway once [Mrs. Z.] couldn't get off at the right
> stop. . . . She says to a big guy with a notebook, a colored fellow,
> Please help me get up. He says to her, You kept me down 300 years,
> you can stay down another ten minutes. I asked her, Nettie, didn't
> you tell him we're raising a little boy brown like a coffee bean. But
> he's right says Nettie, we done that. We kept them down.
>
> We? We? My two sisters and my father were being fried up for
> Hitler's supper in 1944 and you say we?
>
> Nettie sits down. Please bring me some tea. Yes Iz, I say: *We.*
>
> I can't even put up the water I'm so mad. You know, my Mrs.,
> you are crazy like your three aunts, crazy like our Cissy. Your whole
> family put in the genes to make it for sure she wouldn't have a
> chance. Nettie looks at me. She says, Ai, ai. She doesn't say oi any-
> more. She got herself assimilated into ai . . . That's how come she
> also says "we" done it. Don't think this will make you an American,
> I said to her, that you included yourself in with Robert E. Lee.
> Naturally it was a joke, only what is there to laugh? (*LD,* 159–160)

Zagrowsky interprets his wife's acceptance of responsibility for racism as a response to the pressures of assimilation. This is, of course, an arguable interpretation that depends on the belief that accepting responsibility for racism has become a dominant position. But the scene illustrates again the Jewish strategy of joking even while one asks "only what is there to laugh?"

The dominant culture's determination of meaning extends even to definition of what is beautiful, definitions that are easily internalized by muted groups. Faith's father jokes about the effect of such inter-nalized anti-Semitism:

> He had been discussing the slogan "Black is Beautiful" with Chuck
> Johnson, the gatekeeper. Who thought it up, Chuck?

I couldn't tell you, Mr. Darwin. It just settled on the street one day, there it was.

It's brilliant, said Mr. Darwin. If we could've thought that one up, it would've saved a lot of noses, believe me. You know what I'm talking about? (*LD*, 15–16)

Mr. Darwin's joke makes the point that Jewish people have had plastic surgery on their noses not because there was anything wrong with those noses, but because dominant definitions of beauty had muted definitions created from their own reality.

"At That Time, or The History of a Joke" shows how Jewish humor can offer powerful resistance to the pressures of assimilation. Here Paley takes one of the principal tenets of Christian faith, the concept of a virgin birth, and has some fun with it. Setting the story somewhere in the future ("by that time, sexism and racism had no public life, though they were still sometimes practiced by adults at home"), Paley tells of a second virgin birth. This one differs from the Christian version in several important respects. First of all, it comes about because a woman receives a uterus transplant, and the transplanted uterus contains "a darling rolled-up fetus" (*LD*, 94). Thus, this virgin birth has a scientific explanation. In fact, this birth results from scientific technology run amok, for the woman needs a uterus because her "uterus was hysterically ripped from her by a passing gynecologist. He was distracted, he said, by the suffering of a childless couple in Fresh Meadows" (93). (Obviously, the jokes in this short story are relentless, including the pun in the use of the word *hysterically,* a word with Greek origins that originally meant disturbances of the womb. Paley's usage here suggests that the word *hysteria* is the site of yet another exclusionist name based on a reversal.)

Another important difference between this virgin birth and the Christian one is that this time the child is an African American girl, a fact omitted from the initial reports: "'O.K.!' said Dr. Heiliger. 'It's perfectly true, but I didn't want to make waves in any water as viscous as the seas of mythology. Yes, it is a girl. A virgin born of a virgin'" (95). With this revelation, Paley takes a dig at the sexism and racism embedded in beliefs regarding the Christian messiah. When the people in Paley's futuristic tale discover the sex and race of the newborn, they are ready to choose a symbol for celebrating the new

virgin birth: ". . . plans were made to symbolically sew the generations of the daughters to one another by using the holy infant's um-
bilicus. This was luckily flesh *and* symbol. Therefore beside the cross
to which people were accustomed there hung the circle of the navel
and the wiggly line of the umbilical cord" (95). This passage asks the
reader to see the symbolic use of the cross from an outsider's comic
perspective and takes a passing swipe at the Christian belief in a Eu-
charist where symbol (wafer) becomes flesh.

The Jews of the story see this as one more in a long string of false
messiahs. "It is not He! It is not He!" they insist before the child's
sex is announced (a response that becomes a pun when the child's sex
is revealed). Because of the Jews' "stubborn" and "humorless determination," the authorities confiscate all of their electronic means of
communication. They are forced "to visit one another or wander
from town to town in order to say the most ordinary thing to a
friend or relative" (94). In fact, it is through "their gossipy commu-
nications" that the sex of the child becomes known. Nor do they feel
any better about a female messiah: "Wonderful! So? Another tendency heard from! So it's a girl! Praise to the most Highess! But the
fact is, we need another virgin birth like our blessed dead want cup-
ping by ancient holistic practitioners" (95).

Although the Jews of this story are once again constructed as outsiders through the occurrence of a virgin birth (at the story's conclusion they are described as "workers in the muddy basement of history") (96), the actual butt of this joke is the dominant culture and
some of the features of Christianity that appear to Jewish eyes most
absurd. Among these features we might include insistence on the scientific improbability of a virgin birth, attempts to force Jews to
acknowledge Jesus as the messiah, and the commercialization of
Christian symbols throughout the dominant culture ("the birth was
reenacted on giant screens in theaters and on small screens at home")
(94), most notable in the commercialization of Christmas. The resulting "joke" provides the sort of reversal of dominant beliefs (in
this case often achieved by pursuing dominant beliefs to their logical
conclusion or stating the enthymeme) typical of survivalist humor.

Paley's first comic treatment of the problem of assimilation occurs
in one of her earliest stories, "The Loudest Voice." Shirley Abramowitz is chosen to narrate the school's Christmas play because she has

"a particularly loud, clear voice" (*DM*, 56). Her mother is horrified that Shirley and her Jewish classmates are participating in this enactment of the Christian story:

> "I'm surprised to see my neighbors making tra-la-la for Christmas."
>   My father couldn't think of what to say to that. Then he decided: "You're in America! Clara, you wanted to come here. In Palestine the Arabs would be eating you alive. Europe you had pogroms. Argentina is full of Indians. Here you got Christmas. . . . Some joke, ha?" (58)

Mr. Abramowitz's joke argues that there is no place on the globe where Jewish people can live in peace. His comment also suggests that compared with the conflict of the Middle East and the pogroms of Europe, Christmas, despite the pressure to assimilate that the nationwide attention to this holiday exerts, is the least in a list of evils. Finally, by his grim awareness of the reality of this situation he offers resistance to it. Because he sees the situation clearly, he is not yet defeated by it.

He expresses this resistance in another way when Mrs. Kornbluh, mother of the child who played the part of Mary, stops by after the performance for a visit:

> That night Mrs. Kornbluh visited our kitchen for a glass of tea.
>   "How's the virgin?" asked my father with a look of concern.
>   "For a man with a daughter, you got a fresh mouth, Abramovitch."
>   "Here," said my father kindly, "have some lemon, it'll sweeten your disposition." (62)

Here Mr. Abramowitz mocks the Christian belief in a virgin birth, while simultaneously teasing Mrs. Kornbluh and by implication himself as well for their participation in the Christmas pageant. Even when seemingly coopted by the dominant tradition, he maintains his outsider perspective and critique.

In the same conversation, Mrs. Abramowitz reveals that she has also managed to make a distinctly Jewish accommodation to her daughter's participation in the play. Mrs. Kornbluh points out that the Christian children had the smallest parts in the play:

"They got very small parts or no part at all. In very bad taste, it seemed to me. After all, it's their religion."

"Ach," explained my mother, "what could Mr. Hilton do? They got very small voices; after all, why should they holler? The English language they know from the beginning by heart. They're blond like angels. You think it's so important they should get in the play? Christmas . . . the whole piece of goods . . . they own it." (62–63)

By a curious twist of logic, Mrs. Abramowitz has determined that it is more appropriate for the Jewish children to be in the Christmas play than for the Christians. But her analysis has nothing to do with a belief that the Jewish children are or should be part of the dominant group.

"The Loudest Voice" reveals that Shirley has also succeeded in maintaining the double vision available to the outsider who participates as an insider. She notes that the city administration has installed a decorated Christmas tree on one of the corners in the neighborhood and that neighbors are shopping for groceries in a different neighborhood "in order to miss its chilly shadow" while the butcher pulls down "black window shades to keep the colored lights from shining on his chickens." But Shirley has no fears of being tainted by proximity to such Christian symbols: "Oh not me. On the way to school, with both my hands I tossed it a kiss of tolerance. Poor thing, it was a stranger in Egypt" (60). So confident is Shirley in the norms of her Jewish community that she feels free to pity the tree as a shunned outsider. She reiterates this perspective when describing her participation in the play, telling us that she "carefully pronounced all the words about my lonesome childhood." At the end of the day, she listens for a while as her parents and Mrs. Kornbluh discuss the pageant, and then, too sleepy to stay awake any longer, she kneels by her bed: "I made a little church of my hands and said, 'Hear O Israel . . .' . . . I was happy. I fell asleep at once. I had prayed for everybody: my talking family, cousins far away, passersby, and all the lonesome Christians. I expected to be heard. My voice was certainly the loudest" (63). Far from becoming assimilated as a result of her participation in the pageant, Shirley has concluded on the basis of the story she told (the pageant included Jesus' birth, life, and death) that the Christians are a lonesome lot. Furthermore, she knows that if you want to be heard in this world, you have to speak with a loud voice.

By valuing their distinctive perspective as outsiders to the dominant culture, and by continuing to articulate the reality of their experiences with a loud voice, the Jewish characters in Paley's fiction offer a powerful resistance to muteness. Survivalist humor is a crucial element in this resistance, for humor allows them to make clear their conscious awareness of the absurdity inherent in the simultaneously insider/outsider experience of muted groups.

This discussion has isolated three strategies of resistance in Paley's use of Jewish humor: (1) humor in celebration of irrepressible optimism—laughing through one's tears; (2) humor about the absurdity of dominant definitions; and (3) humor as a technique for maintaining an outsider perspective while participating as an insider in the dominant tradition. Paley uses each of these strategies in the service of women as well. Her irrepressible optimism as a strategy for maintaining a woman-centered perspective received lengthy attention earlier in this chapter. The redefinitions catalogued in the preceding chapter offer ample evidence of her use of humor to provide a woman-centered corrective to the absurdity of dominant definitions. As for the third strategy, women more than any other oppressed group have been forced to participate as insiders in a culture that defines us as outsiders, for connections with our oppressors extend beyond work and social life into family and personal life. Thus a humor of resistance that critiques the very culture one participates in becomes a crucial strategy for survival. Just as Shirley Abramowitz comically offers her prayers for "all the lonesome Christians," Paley's women mock male deficiencies. Some of the passages cited in the last chapter offer excellent examples:

> First they make something, then they murder it, then they write a book about how interesting it is. ("The Long-Distance Runner," *EC,* 189)
>
> His time took up with nonsense, you know his conversation got to suffer. A man can't talk. That little minute in his mind most of the time. Once a while busywork, machinery, cars, guns. ("Lavinia: An Old Story," *LD,* 63)
>
> Though I like the attentions as a man he daily give me as a woman, it hardly seemed to tire me as it exhausted him. ("Distance," *EC,* 19)

Perhaps most to the point in its explication of women's fulfillment of our role in the dominant culture while nevertheless maintaining a subversively comic appreciation of our situation is Faith's comment in "The Used-Boy Raisers": "Livid and Pallid were astonished at my outburst, since I rarely express my opinion on any serious matter but only live out my destiny, which is to be, until my expiration date, laughingly the servant of man" (*DM*, 132). Paley has commented on this story as "the beginning of feminism" (see chapter 4). Faith tends to the needs of the two husbands and two sons of this story, but when she tells us that her destiny is to be "laughingly the servant of man," we are left with the strong impression that this is not the laugh of compliance but the laugh of resistance.

Because Paley uses humor liberally in the service of women's resistance to dominant meanings, one could extend these examples considerably. But without belaboring the point, it is clear that Paley has borrowed from a rich Jewish tradition of subversive humor in her woman-centered contradictions of male dominance. Paley has achieved a distinctively female subversive humor by being earthy and earthbound, by being simultaneously realistic and optimistic, and by drawing on the vision available to her as a doubly muted woman to make light of and in women's oppression. What emerges from all of these strategies is the irreverent voice of a survivor.

4
Not Necessarily the End

I didn't want to argue, but I had to say, "Well, it is not necessarily the end, Pa."

—"A CONVERSATION WITH MY FATHER," *EC*, 166

One of the most basic of dominant narrative conventions is the convention of narrative beginning, middle, and end. Unlike life, which continues unfolding without respect to any clear-cut beginning or end point, narrative consists of a story that moves between these two points in time, with the events contained between the beginning and end moments set off from the rest of life and regarded as fixed and completed. Although the story (the implied actual events) unfolds in continuous real time, the narrative may rearrange the chronology of these implied real events and will necessarily select from the events that occurred within the given time period only those pertinent to the concerns of the tale. The types of events deemed worthy of inclusion and the possible narrative resolutions form an important related set of narrative conventions.

Because narrative involves selection and arrangement, narrative choices necessarily express ideology. Rachel Blau DuPlessis calls narrative structures and subjects "working apparatuses of ideology, factories for the 'natural' and 'fantastic' meanings by which we live. Here are produced and disseminated the assumptions, the conflicts, the patterns that create fictional boundaries for experience."[1] Narrative conventions define the patterns of storytelling, providing a structure for stories that support dominance and muting stories that do not fit within their framework: "To compose a work is to negotiate with these questions: what stories can be told? How can plots be resolved? What is felt to be narratable by both literary and social conventions? Indeed, these are issues very acute to certain feminist critics and women writers, with their senses of the untold story, the other side of a well-known tale, the elements of women's existence that have never been revealed."[2] Twentieth-century women writers have participated in "the transgressive invention of narrative strategies, strategies that express critical dissent from dominant narrative."[3]

Narrative Closure in Paley

Because Paley concentrates on telling stories that have not been told before, on stories muted in our language and literature, the dissent from dominant narrative and the transgressive invention of narrative strategies are crucial to her enterprise. This dissent and invention are nowhere more apparent than in her treatment of narrative beginning, middle, and end.

Even the titles of Paley's three volumes of short stories mark her break with dominant narrative conventions. *The Little Disturbances of Man: Stories of Women and Men at Love* signals her attention to the everyday and the ordinary, to subjects usually regarded as too slight to merit literary attention. *Enormous Changes at the Last Minute* reminds us that life, unlike art, is not easily contained within narrative formulae, while *Later the Same Day* suggests a continuation of a story already-in-progress, implying a return to the stories of the first two volumes. In Paley's stories, life is ongoing, eluding the boundaries of dominant narrative forms.

"A Conversation with My Father"

Although subversions of conventional narrative resolutions and a general disregard for the whole notion of narrative resolution and narrative fixity appear throughout Paley's work, her most extensive explicit treatment of these issues occurs in the self-reflexive short story "A Conversation with My Father." This is a story about storytelling. Indeed, "A Conversation with My Father" might almost be named "A Conversation with the (Literary) Patriarchs," for it provides a forum for a discussion of many of the dominant narrative conventions that Paley's fiction subverts. The narrator-author (who seems to have a great deal in common with Paley, including the authorship of "Faith in a Tree" and a father Paley identifies as her own)[4] writes a story in an effort to please her sick father. But even though she tries to please him, she cannot manage to fulfill his requirements for a "simple story, . . . the kind de Maupassant wrote, or Chekhov, the kind you used to write. Just recognizable people and then write down what happened to them next" (*EC*, 161).

The narrator reports that she can't "remember writing that way." Nevertheless, she's willing to try: "I *would* like to try to tell such a story, if he means the kind that begins: 'There was a woman . . .' followed by plot, the absolute line between two points which I've always despised. Not for literary reasons, but because it takes all hope away. Everyone, real or invented, deserves the open destiny of life" (161–162).

Critics have sometimes cited this passage as evidence for the claim that nothing happens in Paley's fiction, a view she disputes:

> I think by writing that story I sort of screwed myself up, because people really don't read. I mean, a great deal happens in almost any one of those stories, really sometimes more than in lots of other peoples', enough to make a novel or something. When people say, well, she really doesn't care much about plot, all they're doing is repeating what I said in my story. Plot is nothing. Plot is only movement in time. If you move in time you have a plot, if you don't move in time, you don't have a plot, you just have a standstill, a painting maybe, or you have something else.[5]

Paley is quite right to point out that plenty happens in her fiction, but what happens often refuses to fit into preexisting (read dominant) narrative formulae, and the text itself refuses to remain fixed within the confines of narrative beginning, middle, and end: "What I *am* against is *thinking* about plot. And it is not the way I write. I just sort of build up a train, and all of a sudden, I look at it and its track. I didn't look for the track to put the train on. And plot does *not* move the story along. People pull you to the next event. Life pulls you. . . . The classical things are really quite marvelous, you know. It's just they have degenerated into a kind of 'well-made-story' of our time."[6]

The story that the narrator of "A Conversation" writes for her father tells of a mother who becomes a junkie in order to keep her teenaged son company, only to be left alone with her habit when her son cleans up and moves away. The first version, only one paragraph long, is rejected by the father because it "left everything out" as

Chekhov and Turgenev would never do. When the daughter asks what it is she has left out, the father questions her about the mother's looks, her parents, and her marital status. The questions are notable for their preoccupation with defining the woman of the story according to key patriarchal categories for women: looks, social status, and marital status. The writer-narrator regards these questions as irrelevant to the tale she wants to tell: "Oh, Pa, this is a simple story about a smart woman who came to N.Y.C. full of interest love trust excitement very up to date, and about her son, what a hard time she had in this world. Married or not, it's of small consequence" (163). But her father cannot agree: "It is of great consequence."

Although she provides answers to her father's questions when he asks, it is significant that this information does not find its way into the revised version of the story. Thus we see her complying on a personal level while maintaining independence within the text that she creates. (It's also interesting to note that throughout her stories Paley ignores such details. For instance, although Faith, her sons, and her friends appear in numerous stories, we know almost nothing about their looks. Nor do we ever learn whether Jack, Faith's companion in the later stories, is her spouse or her live-in boyfriend. These details are important to patriarchal definitions, but they do not interest Paley.)

The revised story, now more than two pages long, is deemed somewhat more acceptable, although the father concludes, "I see you can't tell a plain story. So don't waste time" (166). He is pleased that she has concluded this version with "The End." These words signal to him the fixity of the tale and enable him to assign it to a dominant narrative category: tragedy. His insistence on these points leads to a crucial argument:

> "The end. The end. You were right to put that down. The end."
>
> I didn't want to argue, but I had to say, "Well, it is not necessarily the end, Pa."
>
> "Yes," he said, "what a tragedy. The end of a person."
>
> "No, Pa," I begged him. "It doesn't have to be. She's only about forty. She could be a hundred different things in this world as time goes on. A teacher or a social worker. An ex-junkie! Sometimes it's better than having a master's in education."
>
> "Jokes," he said. "As a writer that's your main trouble. You don't

want to recognize it. Tragedy! Plain tragedy! Historical tragedy! No
hope. The end." (166–167)

The father, with his confidence in dominant narrative structures, insists that the woman's tragic downfall is fixed and final. But the
writer-daughter writes her way past her father's objections:

> I had promised the family to always let him have the last word
> when arguing, but in this case I had a different responsibility. That
> woman lives across the street. She's my knowledge and my in-
> vention. I'm sorry for her. I'm not going to leave her there in that
> house crying. (Actually neither would Life, which unlike me has no
> pity.)
>   Therefore: She did change. Of course her son never came home
> again. But right now, she's the receptionist in a storefront commu-
> nity clinic in the East Village. Most of the customers are young
> people, some old friends. The head doctor has said to her, "If we
> only had three people in this clinic with your experiences . . ." (167)

This passage reveals the connection between Paley's recognition of
the fluidity of life and her resistance to narrative resolution. Her desire to please her father and her deference to his power ("I begged
him") are clear, but the requirements of her fiction are even more
compelling. She respectfully gives her father the story's literal last
word ("How long will it be?" he asked. "Tragedy! You too. When
will you look it in the face?"), but as writer she has already written
her way outside his fixed categories.[7]

"A Conversation" attests to the power of writing to break down
women's muteness. The father can protest to the story's end, but
the narrator-daughter's story has its own life outside the structures
he advocates.

If life is marked by its fluidity, it is not difficult to make a connection between the fixity of dominant male texts and death.[8] To be
fixed, to be beyond change, is to be dead. Thus the traditional insistence on narrative closure can be seen as a denial of life with its inevitable potential for change. DuPlessis notes the contradiction inherent in fiction that chronicles change and choice only to conclude
with finality and fixity: "Having been posed as an experiment in
change and choice, a novel typically ends by asserting that choice is

over and that the growth of character or the capacity for a defining action has ceased. If 'happily ever after' means anything, it means that pleasurable illusion of stasis."[9] Paley, insisting on the stubborn, independent life of her characters,[10] refuses to confine them to the limits of narrative beginning, middle, and end.

Narrative Resolution in
The Little Disturbances of Man

Resistance to conventional narrative resolution occurs even in Paley's earliest work, but the form and the extent of that resistance has undergone development during the course of her thirty-year career. In her first volume, the stories adhere to a number of narrative conventions that subsequent stories will challenge. The beginning, middle, and end of these stories is clearly identifiable; they focus on one particular sequence of events, the protagonist's fortunes change in some recognizable way, and the tale offers a clear sense of narrative resolution. They might be said, in other words, to be more conventionally plotted than many of Paley's later stories (perhaps this is why the father in "A Conversation" speaks wistfully of "a simple story, . . . the kind you used to write").

Nevertheless, these stories offer powerful resistance to the narrative convention that dictates one of two possible resolutions for a female protagonist: marriage or death. DuPlessis observes that, for women, "story . . . has typically meant plots of seduction, courtship, the energies of quest deflected into sexual downfall, the choice of a marriage partner, the melodramas of beginning, middle, and end, the trajectories of sexual arousal and release."[11] This conventional approach places a severe restriction on the scope of a woman's story: "So long as the ending, the completion, of a woman's story is marriage to a man, a woman's adventure will not be a man's adventure. Its time scale will be different, for a woman's adventure will occupy only a small strip of her life, when she is very young."[12] But twentieth-century women writers have undertaken "to solve the contradiction between love and quest and to replace the alternate endings in marriage and death that are their cultural legacy from nineteenth century life and letters by offering a different set of choices."[13]

The Little Disturbances of Man opens with "Goodbye and Good Luck," the story of Rosie's life as told to her niece on the day of her marriage. By ending in Rosie's marriage, this story replays one of the conventional narrative endings for females, but it does so with a degree of self-irony that functions to subvert the power of this outcome.

Although Rosie tells her story to her niece Lillie, she is actually telling Lillie as a means of telling her sister: "So now, darling Lillie, tell this story to your mama from your young mouth. She don't listen to a word from me" (21). The message Rosie has for her sister is that she has finally achieved the traditional happy ending for females: "Tell her after all I'll have a husband, which, as everybody knows, a woman should have at least one before the end of the story" (21).

This statement of narrative resolution has three interesting features. First of all, in its explicit naming of the narrative convention (as well as social convention) that dictates marriage for women, it manifests a consciousness of that convention that undermines its power. Second, the phrase "as everybody knows" suggests that this statement may be somewhat ironic, a suggestion that becomes a certainty with the words "at least one." Obviously, the traditional happy ending in marriage requires that the woman have "at most" one husband rather than "at least" one. Finally, the words "after all" direct our attention to the years of Rosie's life when she chose not to have a husband, preferring instead to follow her heart and maintain her freedom. This marriage is occurring late in her life (she is at least in her fifties). She is marrying a man who in earlier years, while married to another woman, was her lover. She lets her niece know that she had a number of suitors and several marriage proposals. She also supported herself throughout her life.

Although her mother and her sister were horrified by the life she chose, Rosie believes she made the better choice:

> I was popular in certain circles, says Aunt Rose. I wasn't no thinner then, only more stationary in the flesh. In time to come, Lillie, don't be surprised—change is a fact of God. From this no one is excused. Only a person like your mama stands on one foot, she don't notice how big her behind is getting and sings in the canary's ear for thirty years. Who's listening? Papa's in the shop. You and Seymour, thinking about yourself. So she waits in a spotless kitchen for a kind word and thinks—poor Rosie. . . .
>
> Poor Rosie! If there was more life in my little sister, she would

know my heart is a regular college of feelings and there is such information between my corset and me that her whole married life is a
kindergarten. (9)

The energetic Rosie chose quest over marriage and is convinced that
she has been rewarded with a much richer life than the boring and
sterile one her sister elected. Lover for years to a married man, Rosie
should, according to narrative convention, end in ruin. Instead, she
has the excitement and independence of her early years and marriage
for love in her old age. At the end of her tale, she asks Lillie for "a
couple wishes on my wedding day. A long and happy life. Many
years of love" (*DM*, 22). It is clear from the preceding story that she
has already achieved both.

Romantic thralldom and the conventional resolution in marriage
are central to the plot of "A Woman, Young and Old," but once
again the conventional is presented with a twist that subverts its
power. The romantic heroine of "A Woman" is Josephine, a pre-
cocious thirteen-year-old, who paints lipstick on her mouth and
hooks "a wall-eyed brassiere around [her] ribs" in order to capture
the attention of Corporal Brownstar, the boyfriend of her eighteen-
year-old aunt. The day after they meet, she announces their engage-
ment to her family, and by evening's end she has her mother's reluctant blessing. All her plans fall apart, however, when Browny fails to
qualify for a marriage license because his V.D. test is positive. Instead of marrying Josephine, he leaves for camp, "drowned in peni-
cillin and damp with chagrin" (39). Meanwhile, Josie's mother has
managed to meet and marry her (second) true love, despite the fact
that she is still legally married to the first husband who deserted her.
Josie is left to console herself with "the incessant happy noises in
the next room" and the presence of her sister Joanna, "a real cuddly
girl" (40).

"A Woman" undercuts romantic thralldom first of all by presenting a first-person heroine whose age makes her romantic intentions
ridiculous. Josie is so young and inexperienced that when Browny
asks her where she learned to kiss, she innocently replies, "I taught
myself. I practiced on my wrist. See?" (31). Second, the speed of this
romance gives a new meaning to whirlwind affair. In addition, the
impending marriage is ignobly canceled because the groom of this

child bride has V.D. All of these features of the tale tend toward parody of the mystery, glamor, and romance on which plots of romantic thralldom depend.

Finally, the conventional resolution in marriage is replaced by Josephine's cheerful acceptance of the comforts her family of women can provide. Her mother's "incessant happy noises" and her "real cuddly" sister provide satisfactory substitutions for the pleasures she sought with Browny. As her grandmother notes: "Women . . . have been the pleasure and consolation of my entire life" (28). When the grandmother laments the departure of her sons, Josephine seeks to console her with "Ah, Grandma, . . . they were all so grouchy anyway. I don't miss them a bit" (29). One is left with the distinct impression that for Josie, Browny's departure was the happiest of possible narrative resolutions.

Paley frequently writes beyond the conventional ending in marriage by telling the stories of divorced or abandoned women. In "The Pale Pink Roast" Anna encounters her ex-husband, Peter, in the park. He comes home with her to her new apartment where he helps her get settled by hanging blinds and curtains, unpacking books and toys, and sweeping up. This pleasant domestic scene soon leads to lovemaking. Afterward, Peter asks how Anna has managed such a comfortable apartment, and she explains that she has remarried. Peter is furious: "You've made a donkey out of me and him both. . . . Why'd you do it? Revenge? Meanness? Why?" But as Peter heads for the door, Anna explains that she did it "for love" (51). Here again, the resolution of marriage and "happily ever after" is undercut in several ways. For one thing, the existence of ex-husbands is a testimony to the limits of that particular version of "happily ever after." In addition, Anna makes love with Peter for reasons outside of any of the conventional narrative scripts that he suggests—freely and for love. Finally, her choice to make love with her ex-husband even though she is married functions in this case as a challenge to the exclusivity upon which the cultural myth of romantic thralldom depends. Anna is not blind to Peter's faults, as the story clearly indicates, nor does she desire to resume her former relationship with him. She simply chooses to do this today, because it pleases her to do so, and perhaps also in deference to what they once shared.

Virginia, in "An Interest in Life," tells a story that begins when her husband announces that he is deserting her. She is forced to turn to the welfare office and the advice of her neighbors in order to support herself and her three children. Like many of Paley's stories, "An Interest in Life" takes the impermanence of marriage and the undependability of men as givens. Mrs. Raftery offers solace:

> "Look around for comfort, dear." With a nervous finger she pointed to the truckers eating lunch on their haunches across the street, leaning on the loading platforms. She waved her hand to include in all the men marching up and down in search of a decent luncheonette. She didn't leave out the six longshoremen loafing under the fish-market marquee. "If their lungs and stomachs ain't crushed by overwork, they disappear somewhere in the world. Don't be disappointed, Virginia. I don't know a man living'd last you a lifetime." (84)

As pleasant as a woman might find it to have a man around the house, this story argues, she cannot afford to build a life on one. Eventually, Virginia's old friend and former lover, John Raftery, begins to pay her regular Thursday night visits and becomes her lover. The attentions of this kind and gentle married man do not entirely replace her fantasies about the husband who left, but they certainly help her to get through the week.

This story provides an excellent example of what DuPlessis has named "writing beyond the ending." If marriage is the conventional ending for plots about women, this story writes beyond that ending to construct a world in which men are welcome transients and women must take care of themselves.

Two short stories in *The Little Disturbances of Man*, "The Used-Boy Raisers" and "A Subject of Childhood," are included as the two parts of a larger story "Two Short Sad Stories from a Long and Happy Life." This last title provides a frame that directs our attention beyond the incidents of these tales to the knowledge that they are parts in a happier, larger whole. Such a device foreshadows Paley's concern in later volumes with resisting narrative closure and preserving the open-endedness of life. In fact, she goes on in her next two volumes to tell us more about this particular long and happy life, for these are the first two stories that feature Paley's recurrent character Faith.

"The Used-Boy Raisers" writes beyond the traditional resolution in marriage by focusing on a scene with Faith, her current husband, Pallid, and her ex-husband, Livid. As the story begins, Faith is serving breakfast to "the two husbands." They don't like the way she has cooked the eggs, and both sigh "in unison" (127). This opening scene signals the interchangeability of the two men. Even their names, based on each one's appearance at the moment when the eggs are rejected, seem simply to name two different aspects of the same face. At one point, Faith instructs her sons to "Go say goodbye to your father," and the boys ask, "Which one?" (134). Both men feel free to comment on Faith's appearance, "an attractive woman," and to offer advice about the older son's education. During an argument about religion and Israel that unites the two husbands against Faith, one husband says, "When you married *us* . . . didn't you forget about Jerusalem?" (my emphasis, 132). At last Faith urges the two of them to go to work, even though they initially protest that it is Saturday. After shaving together in the bathroom, they agree to split a cab and depart, "clean and neat, rather attractive, shiny men in their thirties, with the grand affairs of the day ahead of them" (134).

Whereas romantic thralldom depends on the notions of exclusivity and the unique qualities of the beloved, this story presents the two "used-boy raisers" as virtual twins. Even the title of the story deconstructs romance as it draws attention to their shared role as surrogate fathers (one, the ex-husband, is the biological father, but his abandonment of the family presumably relegates him to the role of "used-boy raiser" as well). Further, they are defined in this story not in relation to Faith but to her sons. It is almost as if Faith has included these men in her life in order to enlist their help in raising her sons, ineffectual as that help might be. Their departure leaves her free to organize "the greedy day" around the needs of her sons: "dinosaurs in the morning, park in the afternoon, peanut butter in between, and at the end of it all, to reward us for a week of beans endured, a noble rib roast with little onions, dumplings, and pink applesauce" (134).

Despite the difference in temperaments suggested by the names Pallid and Livid, these men are largely indistinguishable in their treatment of and response to Faith. One is left with the strong impression that it would matter little which one returned from work at the end of the day. Faith recognizes that she and the two husbands occupy two different worlds—that the two men have more in common with each other than with her. Paley comments: "That story is the beginning of feminism. Her sense of separation. The idea that her life really is different from the men's. That they are in a world that really was not her concern."[14]

In "The Used-Boy Raisers," Faith works on a piece of embroidery that signals the disruption of traditional family structure and extends the story's powerful critique of marriage as a narrative resolution. While the two husbands breakfast together, Faith stitches a sampler that asks God to "Bless Our Home" (127). "Now as we talked of time past and upon us, I pierced the ranch house that nestles in the shade of a cloud and a Norway maple, just under the golden script" (128). Later in the conversation, Faith reports that her needle is "now deep in the clouds" (132). Faith's traditionally female work on this traditional sampler expresses a nostalgia for a romanticized conventional family life, but when her needle "pierces" a house shadowed by clouds, she provides an obvious metaphor for the disruptions of traditional family arrangements depicted in the story.

The second of these stories, "A Subject of Childhood," occurs a few years prior to "The Used-Boy Raisers." Divorced from her first husband, Faith fights with her boyfriend Clifford because he accuses her of raising her children "lousy." When he leaves, Faith feels "discontinued" and longs for some time alone. She tries to persuade her two little boys to go outside and play. The older son, Richard, finally agrees, but "not because you told me." Tonto, however, resists all her efforts to get him outside, insisting, "I want to stay right next to you. . . . I want to be a baby and stay right next to you every minute. . . . I'm never gonna go away. I'm gonna stay right next to you forever, Faith" (144–145). Tonto crawls into his mother's lap, places his thumb in his mouth, and tells her he loves her:

> "Love," I said. "Oh love, Anthony, I know."
> I held him so and rocked him. I cradled him. I closed my eyes and leaned on his dark head. But the sun in its course emerged among the water towers of downtown office buildings and suddenly shone white and bright on me. Then through the short fat fingers of my son, interred forever, like a black and white barred king in Alcatraz, my heart lit up in stripes. (145)

Here Faith's longing for romance is displaced by her connection to her children, first, because Clifford's attack on her performance as a mother leads to their breakup and, second, Tonto's all-consuming need to be her baby interferes even with her contemplation of the loss of love. The love that Tonto offers both lights up her heart and imprisons her, leaving her literally "a subject of childhood."

All of these stories share a resistance to the narrative resolutions that have dominated fiction about the lives of women. Not one of them presents marriage as the ultimate goal and endpoint in a successful life. Husbands and boyfriends, although often welcome, are unreliable and somewhat transient. Children are much more constant family members in the lives of these women. Although narrative closure is relatively strong in these tales, the types of resolutions possible have undergone significant transformation.

Narrative Resolution in
Enormous Changes at the Last Minute

Paley develops one of her primary challenges to narrative resolution through her creation of characters and situations that recur throughout her three volumes. Although some of Paley's recurrent characters are introduced in her first volume, it is not until *Enormous Changes at the Last Minute* that they reappear and the stories begin to form a web of connection. For instance, Virginia, introduced as narrator of her own tale in "An Interest in Life," is a character in Mrs. Raftery's first-person tale, "Distance." In fact, Mrs. Raftery recounts some of the same events reported earlier by Virginia (providing us with an interesting study in the effects of diverse points of view).[15] The two parts of "Two Short Sad Stories from a Long and Happy Life" introduce Paley's most important recurrent character, Faith, along with Faith's two sons, Richard and Anthony, and Faith's ex-husband Ricardo. In the second collection, these characters recur in "Faith in the Afternoon," "Faith in a Tree," and "The Long-Distance Runner." In addition, Kitty, in "Come On, Ye Sons of Art," snuggles down in her bed under a blanket that is "her friend Faith's grandmother's patchwork quilt" (72). Kitty also makes an appearance in "Faith in a Tree," as do Mrs. Raftery and Anna and Judy (Anna and Judy were introduced in "The Pale Pink Roast" in *The Little Disturbances of Man*). Mrs. Raftery shows up again as Faith's neighbor in "The

Long-Distance Runner." And although she is not named, the female character in "The Immigrant Story" seems to be Faith, since she shares Faith's background and politics and has Jack as her companion (Jack is Faith's boyfriend in "The Long-Distance Runner").

By creating this community of connected characters, Paley again resists the narrative conventions of resolution and fixity. For although the story may end, it ends only to be taken up again at another moment in the character's life. Unlike the serialized novel, which after a number of episodes eventually achieves closure, these short stories featuring recurrent characters provide a structure that continues to elude a final endpoint. The stories create a context for each other, so that it becomes difficult to say just where a particular story begins and ends.

The use of recurrent characters also furnishes a narrative framework for writing about neighborhood and community. The lives of individuals are presented within the context of neighborhood and friendship networks.

This creation of neighborhood extends beyond the stories that explicitly name characters from earlier tales to include all the stories Paley has written. Because the stories are all set in New York and most are set in Greenwich Village, the web of connection that includes Faith and her friends becomes a context even for those stories that do not name these characters. One senses that even when they are not named as participants in a particular situation, they are just around the corner and might at any time walk into the tale.

Critics have sometimes speculated on whether Paley is writing short stories that tend toward the novel, but Paley's form is in fact exactly suited to her purpose. Like the novelist, she creates a world, but it is a world with all the open-endedness and fluidity of life.

Enormous Changes continues Paley's enterprise of writing beyond conventional narrative resolutions. Of the seventeen stories in this volume, eleven include women without husbands. Many of these women are divorced, some are widows, and others are unwed mothers. Three other stories in the volume contain women whose marital status is unknown, and of the three remaining stories, one is about the death of a little boy, one is about the rape and murder of a teenage runaway, and one is about a husband who tries but fails to break out of the static life he is living by having an affair. Thus the volume includes no stories about women whose lives are defined by marriage or the pursuit of marriage. In addition, solidarity between women becomes a significant and explicit concern. As Judith Arcana has noted, "Friendship between women—especially mothers—has become overtly political, inextricable from movement toward social change."[16]

Paley's emphasis on daily life is continued and developed, extending her redefinition of narrative event. Many of these stories seem to have moved about as far as possible from the traditional narrative emphasis on dramatic or unusual events. This is especially true in the extraordinarily short stories (often only two or three pages) that begin to appear in *Enormous Changes*. (These shortest of short stories are a significant part of Paley's challenge to conventions of narrative resolution; in fact, they form such a substantial part of her innovative approach to narrative that I have chosen to reserve them for discussion in the next chapter.)

The title story in *Enormous Changes* not only provides an unconventional resolution but also invents a strategy for presenting this resolution that moves outside the bounds of storytelling convention. During the course of this story, Alexandra, the middle-aged protagonist, becomes pregnant by a much younger man. Her ailing father charges her with embittering his last days and ruining his life, while the young man, Dennis, offers either to bring her and her baby to his commune or to join her in her apartment. The resolution chosen by Alexandra, however, rejects both of these outcomes. Instead, she invites three pregnant clients (she's a social worker) to live with her. They all help each other, the move establishes a precedent in social work, and her father falls in the hospital bathroom and hits his head, conveniently losing some of his memory and recovering "with fewer scruples to notice and appreciate" (135). Dennis continues with his songwriting career, regularly recording songs that celebrate his status as the baby's father.

This narrative resolution offers a significant departure from conventional outcomes for an unwed mother. Alexandra proves to be the agent of her own salvation, creating a community of unwed mothers who furnish each other with a female network of support. But the resolution is interesting not only because it writes a new script, but also because of its narrative structure. Up until the story's resolution, "Enormous Changes" is composed through the juxtaposition of narrative scenes. These scenes alternate between scenes with

Alexandra and Dennis in the taxi or the apartment and scenes with Alexandra and her father in the hospital. At the story's conclusion, however, the narrator announces: "This is what Alexandra did in order to make good use of the events of her life" (134). The rest of the story consists of a summary of the concluding events described above. Scenic presentation is over. This narrative summary almost seems to exist outside the parameters of the story that precedes it. One is reminded strongly of the added-on ending to the daughter's story in "A Conversation with My Father." The scenic presentation of this tale ends with Dennis's announcement, "In that case, this is it, I'm splitting" (134). That might be an appropriate final moment for a more conventional narrative. But it cannot contain the resourcefulness of an Alexandra who intends "to make good use of the events of her life."

The final story in this volume, "The Long-Distance Runner," also diverges from dominant notions of narrative event. A middle-aged Faith takes up jogging, says goodbye to her sons, and runs off to her childhood neighborhood. Here, in what has now become a predominantly African American neighborhood, she takes up residence for three weeks in her former apartment with Mrs. Luddy, Mrs. Luddy's son Donald, and three baby girls. In this altered landscape of her childhood, Faith's well-meaning liberalism is challenged.

Her first guide is the girl scout Cynthia, who takes her into her old apartment building. When Faith learns that her former neighbor, Mrs. Goreditsky, died only two years earlier, she is surprised:

> Only two years ago. She was still here! Wasn't she scared?
> So we all, said Cynthia. White ain't everything. (185)

A few moments later, they pass the apartment once occupied by Faith's best friend. Faith begins to tell Cynthia what has become of her and her wealthy husband. Cynthia's ironic comment is simply "Different spokes for different folks" (185).

Faith is eventually chased by some angry boys who think she is trying to bother Cynthia. She takes refuge in her childhood apartment. Once settled, she finds herself reluctant to leave its safety: "I'd get to the door and then I'd hear voices. I'm ashamed to say I'd become fearful. Despite my wide geographical love of mankind, I would be attacked by local fears" (188).

Faith's "wide geographical love of mankind" is precisely what her journey to her old neighborhood challenges. She continues throughout her visit to reveal her good intentions and her limited awareness. Surveying the decay of the neighborhood, she announces, "Someone ought to clean that up." Mrs. Luddy sarcastically asks "who you got in mind? Mrs. Kennedy?" (190).

Despite Faith's blunders, she and Mrs. Luddy manage to achieve a connection as they diaper the babies, talk with Donald, and share information about simple pleasures for hard times and observations about life and men. At last Mrs. Luddy announces that it is time for Faith to leave ("This ain't Free Vacation Farm") and Faith jogs away, now in possession of a more realistic view of the diversity and complexity of the world and the limitations of her own experience and perspective.

At home she tries to tell her family about her experience, but she has trouble getting them to understand what has happened to her. Richard says, "What are you talking about?" Later Anthony listens for a while and concludes, "I don't know what she's talking about either." Even Jack, "despite the understanding often produced by love after absence," can't get it:

> He said, Tell me again. He was in a good mood. He said, You can even tell it to me twice.
>
> I repeated the story. They all said, What? (198)

Faith's story provides a radical departure from dominant structures of meaning. Although she knows something important has happened in her life, she cannot find a way to communicate it to Jack and her sons. Finally, in her attempt to find someone who can comprehend the significance of her quest, she appeals to the reader: "Because it isn't usually so simple. Have you known it to happen much nowadays? A woman inside the steamy energy of middle age runs and runs. She finds the houses and streets where her childhood happened. She lives in them. She learns as though she was a child what in the world is coming next" (198).

Narrative Resolution in *Later the Same Day*

Paley's most recent volume of short stories, *Later the Same Day,* continues and expands her innovative approach to narrative beginning, middle, and end. As always, the stories that Paley tells come from a territory at the margins of dominant culture. For instance, old friendships between groups of middle-aged women are featured. Judith Arcana identifies women's friendship as a primary theme in three of this volume's stories ("Ruthy and Edie," "The Expensive Moment," and "Friends") and a prominent theme in two more ("Love" and "Listening"), while two other stories feature groups of women friends ("Somewhere Else" and "Zagrowsky Tells"). [17] As a matter of fact, women in middle-age get much more attention in this volume than they have usually received in the pages of literature.

The network of Faith stories continues, including at least eight of the seventeen stories in this volume (some stories, such as "Love" and "Anxiety," do not name any of the characters from the Faith stories but nevertheless seem to partake of the same cultural milieu—the eight counted above explicitly name Faith or her friends).

Because the women are growing older, their neighborhood has expanded to include a larger part of the world. This movement into a larger world results from political concerns that have moved beyond the block and the P.T.A. to the globe, from increased opportunities to travel to other countries, and from the expanded movement of their grown or nearly grown children.

Besides continuing the development of previously developed transgressive narrative strategies, Paley also invents some new techniques in this volume for resisting narrative closure and fixity. Three of the stories from *Later the Same Day* can serve as examples of some of Paley's narrative innovations in this stage of her career.

The narrator-protagonist of "Love" announces to her husband that she has "just written a poem about love" (3). This leads him to reflect on various loves of his life. The last name in his list surprises his wife:

> When at last he came to my time—that is, the last fifteen years or so—he told me about Dotty Wasserman.
>
> Hold on, I said. What do you mean, Dotty Wasserman? She's a character in a book. She's not even a person. (4)

Dotty Wasserman is, in fact, a character in one of Paley's early stories, "The Contest." She appears again briefly in "Faith in a Tree" when a letter from Faith's ex-husband Ricardo names her as his current living companion.

Despite the narrator's protests, her husband continues to insist that Dotty Wasserman is part of his history, inventing stories of their time together:

> No, I said, that's not true. She was made up, just plain invented in the late fifties.
> Oh, he said, then it was after that. I must have met her afterward. (5)

The narrator decides to drop the subject, although later she muses about its relationship to her thoughts about love: "How interesting the way [love] glides to solid invented figures from true remembered wraiths. By God, I thought, the lover is real. The heart of the lover continues; it has been propagandized from birth" (5–6). While her mind has considered the "true remembered wraiths" she has loved, her husband has been attending to the "solid invented figure" of Dotty Wasserman. His insistence on Dotty's reality becomes the last word of the text, when he announces to his wife: "You're some lover, you know . . . You really are. You remind me a lot of Dotty Wasserman" (7).

This sort of self-reflexive playing with the boundaries between the fictive and the real world offers a significant challenge to narrative closure. The story as a self-contained (and lifelike) world is challenged through this transgression of the distinction between fiction and reality. Paley's characters have become so real that now a husband (one is tempted to say her husband, for the distinction between this narrator-character and Paley is so slight as to seem to disappear) is claiming one of them as an ex-lover. The complexity of this claim is compounded by the fact that the claimant is himself a fictive character. The narrator seems to work all this out for herself by noting the interesting way love "glides to solid invented figures from true remembered wraiths." But the reader is left with a text that strongly resists closure.

"Love" undermines closure in another way by including information about an occurrence three years after this story's conclusion: "I passed our local bookstore, which was doing well, with *The Joy of All Sex* underpinning its prosperity. The owner gave me, a dependable customer of poorly advertised books, an affectionate smile. He was a great success. (He didn't know that three years later his rent would be tripled, he would become a sad failure, and the landlord, feeling himself brilliant, an outwitting entrepreneur, a star in the micro-economic heavens, would be the famous success.)" (6). Although the fortunes of the bookstore owner are peripheral to this particular story, this parenthetical information serves to remind us that the fixity of any text is illusory, for the characters are not frozen in the moment of resolution. Life goes on, and with it go the inevitable and unexpected changes in fortune.

The final challenge the story poses to conventional treatment of narrative beginning, middle, and end occurs through its almost associative or thematic structure. After the narrator writes a poem about love, tells her husband about it, and hears about the loves of his life, including Dotty Wasserman, she walks to the grocery musing about love. She sees the kale in the grocer's bin, invents a new poem about kale, and then encounters an old friend, Margaret, who hasn't spoken to her in two years:

> We'd had many years of political agreement before some matters re-
> lating to the Soviet Union separated us. In the angry months during
> which we were both right in many ways, she took away with her to
> her political position and daily friendship my own best friend,
> Louise—my lifelong park, P.T.A., and antiwar-movement sister,
> Louise.
> In a hazy litter of love and leafy green vegetables I saw Margaret's
> good face, and before I remembered our serious difference, I smiled.
> At the same moment, she knew me and smiled. So foolish is the true
> lover when responded to that I took her hand as we passed, bent to
> it, pressed it to my cheek, and touched it with my lips. (6–7)

Up until this moment, the story focuses on romantic love. With this incident, we move to a wider definition and consideration of love, the lover, and the beloved. The husband explains the wife's actions to her: "Don't you know? The smile was for Margaret but really you do miss Louise a lot and the kiss was for Louise" (7). The two then spend a companionable evening together and end by making love. This technique of moving between scenes according to their ability to elaborate on a theme or topic rather than because they move in some sort of linear causal chain toward the moment of the story's climax will be the object of further investigation when we turn to the final story in this volume, "Listening" (and again in chapter 5).

"The Story Hearer" deals explicitly with problems of beginning, middle, and end. When Jack asks the narrator, Faith, what she did with her day, and she inquires, "Shall we begin at the beginning?" the problem of beginning, of finding the beginning moment, is posed immediately. The question also delays the beginning of Faith's story, for a discussion of preferences regarding beginnings and middles and an interjection from Jack about his sad childhood follow. A page or so later, Faith tries again: "Therefore I want to go on with the story. Or perhaps begin it again. Jack said, what did you do today with your year off? I said . . ." (134). The ambiguous status of this story's beginning is attested to in the first two of these lines. When Faith starts over, is she going on with her story or beginning again? And what exactly is the beginning moment? The moment when she begins her account of her day? Or the moment when she begins telling us about her conversation with Jack?

Like "Love," "The Story Hearer" also contains a challenge to narrative closure in the form of a flash-forward two years beyond the time of the story. Faith is chatting amiably with the grocer. Then she tells us: "A couple of years later—in the present, which I have not quite mentioned (but will)—we fought over Chilean plums. We parted. I was forced to shop in the reasonable supermarket among disinterested people with no credit asked and none offered. But at that particular moment we were at peace. That is, I owed him $275 and he allowed it" (141). Faith's parenthetical "but will" serves to remind us that her storytelling is an ongoing project. She has not yet told us the stories of the present moment, but she will.

At the end of Faith's story to Jack, she realizes that "the day had been too long and I hadn't said one word about the New Young Fathers or my meeting with Zagrowsky the Pharmacist. I thought we might discuss them at breakfast" (142). There are two interesting features to this passage. First, it refers outside this story to others in the volume. "Zagrowsky Tells" gives his version of the meeting with Faith. "The New Young Fathers" might be a reference to "Anxiety," in which a narrator much like Faith leans out her window to reprimand a couple of young fathers. Such references remind the reader of the many possible narrative renderings of any story and again resist closure.

Faith's comment that the day has been too long also refers to the process of selection and arrangement whereby events are structured into stories. She acknowledges, with this remark, the impossibility of giving a complete account of the events in any given story's sequence of events. Thus, she comments not only on the difficulties of finding a story's endpoint but also on the problem of determining exactly what events should constitute the middle. If the storyteller tries to include everything, she may never reach the end.

The end of Faith's daytime story is not the end of "The Story Hearer," a discrepancy that poses again issues related to the clear determination of beginning, middle, and end. Faith and Jack go to sleep, but Faith, after a frightening dream, wakes Jack with the storyteller's call: "I want to tell you something, Jack" (143). What she wants to tell him is that she wants to have a baby. He informs her that she's "a couple years too late." He then falls asleep but continues to discuss the problem with her. Thus, his role as story hearer extends even into sleep. The story concludes with Faith's reply: "I'm with you there . . . Now all you have to do is be with me." Perhaps being with each other is a large measure of what this business of storytelling and story hearing is about.

"Listening" provides the best example from Paley's work of the kind of associative or thematic pattern of organization described above with reference to "Love." Because this story is the object of considerable discussion in chapter 6 we will look at it somewhat briefly here.

"Listening" consists of three scenes, two one day apart and the third occurring several years later. In the first scene, Faith sits in a deli and overhears a couple of conversations. When she later tells Jack about this, he reveals what Faith already knew but the reader did not: he was one of the people she overheard. As the scene continues, Jack appeals to Faith at one juncture with the words, "Listen. Listen." Later Richard, "known far and wide for his nosy ear," comments to Faith on a part of their conversation he has overheard. The final scene, several years later, occurs between Faith and her friend Cassie, and provides a profound critique of Faith's capacity as a listener. These scenes are not united in the conventional way—by a linear plot that pursues causal connections. Instead, they are linked thematically by their relationship to the topic of listening. Each scene offers different insights into or comments upon the subject of listening. This constitutes yet another rupture of conventional approaches to narrative closure.

The resistance to narrative closure and fixity apparent throughout Paley's work insists on the connection of any single event to the whole of life and to a complex web of connections between people. Life is full of interruptions, changes, and surprising twists and turns, always resisting any attempt on our part to control it by asserting, now it is finished. In addition, Paley's work argues that a story need not concern itself with moments of great dramatic tension, powerfully built toward and then released in a climactic moment. It is enough to juxtapose two or three scenes, persons, ideas, or experiences in a context where they can comment on and illumine one another. This quietly revolutionary approach to storytelling opens up a space for a multitude of previously untold stories.

5

As Simply as Possible

It was possible that I did owe something to my own family and the families of my friends. That is to tell their stories as simply as possible, in order you might say, to save a few lives.

—"DEBTS," *EC*, 10

A s a short story writer, Paley is already one step outside the literary mainstream, which subscribes to a bigger-is-better aesthetics, positing the novel as the appropriate site of serious literary critical attention.[1] One can aspire to write the Great American Novel, but creating the Great American Short Story is not a similarly valued goal. Paley adds to her marginalized status as a woman and a Jew by choosing to write short stories. In her second and third volumes, she compounds this triply marginal status by writing short stories of such brevity that they sometimes seem to be seeking the minimal limits of the genre. These shortest stories have consistently attracted negative criticism. Yet the charge that these works fail to conform to the limits of the short story genre provides one measure of the extent to which they serve as a challenge and a corrective to dominant narrative structures.

Reviewers and critics have tended to regard the shortest stories as her weakest work. These pieces are described as "underpowered," "quizzical wisps of an idea or situation which is not always fully rounded or developed," "short and written within an inch of their lives," "little more than nervous, haphazard sketches about ill-defined people."[2] The scolding critics echo the father in "A Conversation with My Father" complaining of his daughter's inability to "tell a plain story" and her tendency to leave "everything out" (*EC*, 166, 162).

In fact, many of the characteristics that so irritate the critics in her shortest stories are simply more concentrated presentations of features that appear in her longer stories as well. One begins to suspect that the critics' identification of the shortness of these works as the locus of the problem is a red herring.

If we assume, as Paley does, that these shortest stories are central to her work rather than examples of what happens when her craft lapses, then the critical disapproval (or alternatively, silence) they have attracted suggests that they might provide particularly fruitful ground for identifying how Paley throughout her corpus revises narrative structure in order to make space in the dominant discourse for woman-centered stories. From the perspective of the dominant tradition, Paley's shortest stories may look like failures. But this chapter argues that while Paley's work always exists in a dialogic relationship with the dominant tradition, it draws a large measure of its vitality and originality from a much older oral tradition: the tradition of women's personal narratives. This tradition equips Paley with narrative strategies that permit her to tell stories "untellable" according to the criteria of the dominant (male) literary tradition. In tracing the connections between women's personal narratives and Paley's short stories, I will begin with a summary of the distinctive characteristics of women's personal narratives, move to Paley's own acknowledgment of orality in general comments on her shortest stories, and finally examine the stories themselves for evidence of this tradition.

Connections to Women's Personal Narratives

Paley draws on the lively oral tradition of her own Jewish culture. Her emphasis on orality is illustrated by her method of composition—she reads her work aloud while writing to find out if it sounds right; her method of teaching writing—she has her students read their stories to each other without distributing manuscripts and holds informal poetry readings in her office; and her personal life—she remains extraordinarily accessible by phone to both friends and strangers, and the telephone's ring frequently punctuates any conversation she has in her home.[3] With an author so attuned to orality and so focused on the lives of women, it makes sense to look for connections between Paley's narrative structure and the structures of women's personal narratives.

Women's personal narratives are oral stories told by women about our own experiences. It is not surprising to learn that women's narratives have often been evaluated as deficient in some respect, failing to meet the dominant criteria for "tellability" and a "well-formed" story. In a review of the empirical research literature examining women's personal narratives, Kristin Langellier has identified six characteristics that distinguish women's narratives from dominant models of storytelling.

First, women's narratives may not be "tellable" according to the dominant expectation of personal narratives structured by a remarkable event or action. Instead, women's stories tend to focus on commonplace events, typical or usual circumstances, or stories of emotional rather than dramatic interest. Second, women's stories may differ structurally from the dominant model. For instance. women may tell "non-linear, open-ended stories of descriptive detail that are not marked off from the surrounding conversation." Third, women often collaborate as storytellers, telling stories as a group rather than as individuals. Fourth, women may tell stories "for the purpose of self-sharing rather than self-enhancement. . . . Women's personal narratives bond women as women in their similar experiences and shared meanings." Fifth, women's personal narratives may not "make a point" (personal narrative research refers to this as the evaluative function). The point of women's narratives may change, be negotiated, or even be "unknown in the act of telling." Women's personal narratives "search for (rather than take for granted) and discover (rather than reify) culturally interesting materials for women's experiences." "Sense-making" takes precedence over "point-making." Sixth, women's stories "may be sex-specific and context-specific." That is, some of these stories may be told only to other women in private rather than public settings (dominant narratives can be told in private *and* public settings).[4]

Paley on Her Shortest Stories

Paley's own discussions of her shortest stories offer a useful point of entry to an exploration of the influence of women's personal narratives on her work. Interviewers have questioned Paley repeatedly about her shortest pieces. When Joan Lidoff asked, "Can a story be too short?" Paley replied: "More often it's too long. . . . A story is for me . . . the word 'conflict' is often used, and I don't really like that word; maybe it's because I'm a pacifist or whatever reason. I think it's just a more simple dialectic than that. I think it's two events or two characters or two winds or two different ideas or whatever, bumping into each other, and what you hear, that's the story. And that can happen in two pages."[5] The notion that story can emerge from a simple dialectic that need not be expressed in full-scale conflict stands in contrast to the male tradition of a successful story: "In what most of us consider a successful story, the beginning states or establishes the grounds for conflicts that the ending resolves."[6] But Paley's explanation coincides with a women's oral tradition that emphasizes the ordinary and eschews large-scale drama.

Quite willing to redefine essential components of narrative in order to accommodate the stories that interest her, Paley also manifests a disdain for traditional genre distinctions: "I think we worry too much about what form is which. I've noticed that heavy fiction people really don't like those little one-page two-page stories. I mean the reviewers, the fiction reviewers. Now if it's poetry reviewers, they usually like them, but if they're fiction reviewers they usually say 'This thing wasn't developed, you know. Why doesn't it go somewhere?'"[7] Paley links the form of these stories and the form of poetry: "I think my shortness comes also from my having written poetry. Poetry is closer to the short story."[8] We are not surprised when a poem provides a brief glimpse that illumines a whole life, but such an approach is unusual in short stories.

Paley offers further explanations of her brevity:

That comes from starting to write later in life. Time goes by so fast. And I think you *can* cover a lot in a short period of time. It's one of the gifts of the short story. I don't think you need transitions. You're taught about transitions, but you don't need them. People's imagination has been changed by watching television. You sit and look at some TV shows, some of the worst, some of the cheapest, and you'll see them do technical tricks with time that Don (Barthelme), Coover, Barth, and everybody rolled into one would be terrified to do. . . . It's just that any more information in my stories would be extraneous and boring and only make the work much longer than it needs to be.[9]

She makes a similar point more succinctly and with characteristic wit when she explains that her shortness is "because art is too long and life is too short."[10]

What appears to some critics as a failure to "flesh out" her characters is to Paley an achievement of simplicity. Her emphasis on the connection between her writing and the oral tradition on which it draws is explicit in her description of herself as a storyteller rather than a writer and her eschewing of the word *fiction* in favor of *stories*.[11] Paley has remarked, "I want to be a story-teller when I grow down. But I believe we are all story-tellers."[12] In "Debts," the narrator articulates Paley's project: "It was possible that I did owe something to my own family and the families of my friends. That is, to tell their stories as simply as possible, in order, you might say, to save a few lives" (*EC,* 10). This passage relates her emphasis on simplicity to her interest in presenting the daily lives of her family and friends. She writes these simple stories in order to memorialize.

Her stories regularly voice this concern with recording the lives of her friends: "He was right to call my attention to [the world's] suffering and danger. He was right to harass my responsible nature. But I was right to invent for my friends and our children a report on these private deaths and the condition of our lifelong attachments" ("Friends," *LD,* 89). Paley explains her storytelling impulse this way: "I write for my friends, to tell the stories of their lives."[13]

These are simple stories because they are the stories women might choose to tell each other about our daily lives: "I think a lot of story telling really comes from 'I want to tell you something.' Almost all stories come from that. From the very first time you walk into a house and say 'I want to tell you something.' That story 'Friends' I really wrote for my friends; I hoped that they would read it. I wrote it toward them and also from them."[14]

In fact, Paley's work offers precise parallels to each of the six distinguishing characteristics of women's oral narrative identified by Langellier:

1. Paley's stories violate criteria for "tellability," focusing on commonplace events, typical or usual circumstances, and stories of emotional rather than dramatic interest.
2. Paley's stories are often nonlinear and open-ended, less clearly

marked off through narrative closure from surrounding life than
is traditional fiction.

3. As I will argue in the next chapter, Paley often engages in collaborative storytelling, allowing characters to interrupt, amend,
and extend the narrator's account of events.[15]

4. Paley tells stories in order to share, to read into the record, the
lives and experiences of women, "illuminating what's hidden."

5. Paley's stories are frequently indicted by critics for their failure
to make a point, but Paley claims that she writes in order "to
understand."

6. Paley's stories are often the type women tell each other around
the kitchen table. As Faith says to Jack when he asks her to tell
him "stories told by women about women," "Those are too private" ("Listening," *LD*, 203).

Paley, in listing the reasons for writing, summarizes several of these
points: "You write to say I want to tell you something on the sim-
plest level. You write to say I don't understand this. I'm going to try
to understand it. I don't know. You write to memorialize certain
things and people, to remember them. And you write really in praise
as well as in fear. The knock wood stories."[16]

This remarkable degree of correlation makes it clear that Paley has
drawn on a tradition of women's personal narratives in developing
strategies for "illuminating what's hidden," for telling in the public
forum of literature stories that have previously been confined to the
privacy of a female oral culture. Thus, she articulates the muted by
insisting that previously muted structures deserve attention, not only
in the privacy of the kitchen but even when placed in a dominant
(public) context—that is, literature. Although the correlations between characteristics of women's personal narratives and strategies in
Paley's stories illuminate all her works, they prove particularly helpful in expanding our understanding of what she is doing in some of
her briefest stories.

Enormous Changes at the Last Minute

One of the ways Paley subverts conventional expectations about narrative is through inscribing unconventional notions of what constitutes narrative event. Her emphasis on the daily lives of women and

children and her concern with telling the stories of ordinary people are aspects of this redefinition of narrative event. But even readers who have grown accustomed to the idea that ordinary women and children may be fit subjects for narrative sometimes respond to Paley's short stories by wondering, "What happened?" In "Wants," story time from beginning to end is only a few minutes. During those minutes, the protagonist-narrator encounters her ex-husband outside the library, they talk, she rechecks two long-overdue books, he insults her, she sits down on the steps to think, and then she returns the rechecked library books. Stated in these terms, story event seems to be so slight that it scarcely conforms to notions of what constitutes a story. But Paley's protagonist, in these few moments, achieves insight into the disparity between her and her ex-husband's ambitions and a clearer understanding of her own desires.

The ex-husband is looking for trouble. He challenges her greeting of "Hello, my life," with "What? What life? No life of mine." He then follows her into the library to offer an accusation: "In many ways, he said, as I look back, I attribute the dissolution of our marriage to the fact that you never invited the Bertrams to dinner" (3–4). This explanation is so absurdly trivial that one expects the protagonist to dismiss it outright. But instead she responds with a causal chain that reveals typical Paley awareness of how the large and small events of life combine to interrupt and distract us from an original intention: "That's possible, I said. But really, if you remember, first, my father was sick that Friday, then the children were born, then I had those Tuesday-night meetings, then the war began. Then we didn't seem to know them anymore. But you're right. I should have had them to dinner" (4). Having failed to provoke a fight with his first accusation, the ex-husband goes on to charge her with not having wanted anything. He points out that he is doing well, putting "money down on an eighteen-foot two-rigger. . . . But as for you, it's too late. You'll always want nothing" (5).

Stung by this remark, the narrator sits down to think over her shortage "of requests and absolute requirements." She discovers that she does "want *something*." Her list includes becoming a different person, returning her books on time, becoming an effective advocate for the school system and the city, ending the war for her children, and remaining married forever to one person (since she is already in her second marriage, this desire is as impossible as her wish to be a different person). Determined to prove that she can take action, she chooses the most performable item in her list and returns her books.

The wants of a person without any particular material requirements are not as easily expressed or understood through the language of a materialist culture as the wants of someone who longs for "an eighteen-foot two-rigger." How can you explain the desire for good schools, socially active citizens, world peace, and enduring commitments in the language of consumerism? Something happens in this story, but it is the something of introspection and self-awareness rather than the something of public and heroic action. Emotional interest is stronger than dramatic interest, and the story concerns itself with understanding the wants of its narrator-protagonist rather than with making a point.

"Living" and "Northeast Playground" are two other stories in *Enormous Changes* that can be seen as redefining what constitutes narrative event. In one sense, "Living" might seem an unlikely candidate for this category, for in it, Faith's friend Ellen dies and Faith herself is so sick she believes she is dying, too. That sounds like plenty of plot. But the focus of the three-page story is Faith's connection with her friend and the extent to which they have shared their lives and, in some sense, even their deaths. Such connection occurs despite the terrors and displacements of a modern world in which "You have to be cockeyed to love, and blind in order to look out the window at your own ice-cold street" (59). Thus this brief tale shuns the dramatic (life and death) as well as the rigors of modernist despair in favor of the simply human and particularly female: two women whose friendship makes living and dying into a collaborative venture.

In "Northeast Playground" a narrator who is probably Faith reports on finding "eleven unwed mothers on relief" assembled with their children at the playground. The conversation between the narrator and the mothers explores the differences between the mothers' solidarity and the experience the narrator had when her children were small: "when I was a mother of babies in this same park, we were not so unified and often quarreled, accusing other children of unhealthy aggression or excessive timidity. He's a ruined wreck, we'd say about some streaky squeaker about two years old. No hope. His eyelids droop. Look how he hangs on to his little armored prick!"

(146). Yet similarities exist as well. The unwed mothers do not mix with the married mothers, just as in the narrator's days in the park: "The ladies who once wore "I Like Ike" buttons sat on the south side of the sandbox, and the rest of us who were revisionist Communist and revisionist Trotskyite and revisionist Zionist registered Democrats sat on the north side" (148).

Judith Arcana has called these unwed mothers "a model support group."[17] Certainly this story draws attention to the way mothers, assembled together on playgrounds, have formed connections with and provided support for one another. The reference to two generations of mothers also points to the continuity of such connections between women while acknowledging the changes that have occurred. In terms of conventional narrative, nothing happens in this story. Yet we are given a glimpse of a part of women's lives that has heretofore been hidden.

At times her stories are so simple in their construction that the very simplicity interferes with our ability to recognize their characters according to our conventional categories. "Debts" is the story in which the narrator announces that she has decided she owes it to her family and the families of her friends "to tell their stories as simply as possible" (10). What follows is a two-page story of Maria and Lucia. The story tells us a great deal about the difficult events of Lucia's and Maria's lives. However, it offers such a skeletal summary of these events that it recalls the complaint of the father, "You left everything out."

Yet the frame for this tale provides the context for understanding its structure. The narrator reports that a woman called and asked her to "help her write about her grandfather, a famous innovator and dreamer of the Yiddish theater" (9). She refuses ("I had already used every single thing I knew about the Yiddish theater to write one story, and I didn't have time to learn any more, then write about it").[18] Later she discusses the incident with her friend Lucia, who explains "that it was probably hard to have family archives or even only stories about outstanding grandparents or uncles when one was sixty or seventy and there was no writer in the family and the children were in the middle of their own lives. She said it was a pity to lose all this inheritance just because of one's own mortality" (9–10). Having decided to "save a few lives," the narrator begins the story with this explanation: "Because it was her idea, the first story is Lucia's. I tell it so that some people will remember Lucia's grandmother, also her mother, who in this story is eight or nine" (10).

In telling the story of Maria and Anna, Paley is telling a family story of the sort passed from one generation to the next. If we remember her concern with "illuminating what's hidden," with simply getting the lives of women on the record, and with memorializing, it becomes clear that the point here is not to make a point but simply to preserve a story about an ordinarily resourceful woman who manages despite hard times. This is a story "told by women about women." In addition, the story is for Lucia, who no doubt can understand her own life better because she knows this story about her mother and her grandmother.

Three other stories in *Enormous Changes* provide extraordinarily compressed accounts of action-packed stories. "Gloomy Tune" tells in three and a half pages how Yoyo became known throughout the neighborhood "for using a knife." He has become a neighborhood character, as the story's conclusion reveals: "In school he gets prayed for every day by all the kids, boys or girls" (56). The language in "Gloomy Tune" is oral and colloquial. "There is a family . . . ," the story begins, invoking a formulaic beginning for an oral narrative. The simple (and often parallel) sentence structure and use of slang further reinforce this impression of orality:

> They are very narrow-minded. They never have an idea. But they like to be right. They never listen to anyone else's ideas.
> One after another, Dodo, Neddy, Yoyo, and Put Put got the sisters at the school into a state. The sisters had to give up on them and they got dumped where they belonged for being fresh: right in the public school. (53)

The narrator sounds like one of Yoyo's neighbors, explaining to a newcomer how Yoyo got his reputation as a troublemaker. In such a tale, the need for scenic detail and elaborate description is slight.

"Samuel" explores in just over three pages the death of a little boy who is playing with his friends "on the platform between the locked doors of the subway cars." In its few paragraphs, this story investigates the reactions of the women and men on the subway who see the boys playing, the attitudes of the boys themselves, and the response of Samuel's parents, especially his mother. The parents go on to have other children, only to realize that "never again will a boy exactly like Samuel be known" (106). Covering so much territory in such a short space results in significant compression. Distinct characters are replaced by collective groups. The boys, virtually indistinguishable from one another except in the moment when Samuel pitches to his death, collectively jump and jiggle, "jerk forward and backward and grab the swinging guard chains," and "pound each other's back" in laughter (104–105). The men on the train who watch the boys form a second group, again presented collectively: "These two men and others looked at the four boys jumping and jiggling on the platform and thought, It must be fun to ride that way, especially now the weather is nice and we're out of the tunnel and way high over the Bronx. Then they thought, These kids do seem to be acting sort of stupid. They *are* little. Then they thought of some of the brave things they had done when they were boys and jiggling didn't seem so risky" (104). "The ladies" comprise a third collectively portrayed group, becoming "very angry when they looked at the four boys" (104). After the accident: "The ladies waited around wondering if he might be an only child. The men recalled other afternoons with similar bad endings. The little boys stayed close to each other, leaning and touching shoulders and arms and legs" (106). All of this collectivity seems to work in opposition to the mother's concluding realization that "never again will a boy exactly like Samuel be known." But this is at least part of the point of this compressed exploration of Samuel's death. In her recognition that her new son cannot replace her lost Samuel, Samuel's mother is in the paradoxical position of being Everymother as she acknowledges that each human life is unique. The goal of such a story has nothing to do with conventional explorations of character or depictions of unique events. Instead, Paley is exploring a category of catastrophe that surely forms the stuff of every mother's nightmares. For children are heedless of their own mortality, and although most somehow manage to survive anyway, a few do not. Paley speaks of her attempt to understand this event by writing about it:

> If I'm going to write something about a kid dying, I'm really doing
> a couple of things. I'm knocking wood about such an event. 'Cause
> it's totally invented, and yet could happen every day, and probably

has happened several times in the New York subways. And I'm investigating something. I'm trying to understand what that event is.
And what it is to the people around it. What it is to the other little
boys. What it is to the motor man. What it is to the women. And
what it is mostly to the mother. What that loss is. So I'm trying to
understand.[19]

This story provides an excellent example of an attempt through narrative to search for sense rather than to make a point.

Paley has described both "Samuel" and "The Burdened Man" as
"pure plot" (37). "The Burdened Man" tells the story of a man's life
in six pages. According to Paley, "It's about a guy who has a very
narrow life, which he widens for one minute . . ." (36). Again, individual character distinctions are replaced by generic descriptions.
The title is itself generic, and the protagonist continues to be known
as "the man" or "he" throughout the story. Other characters are "his
son," "his wife," "the woman," and "the husband." As with "Samuel," such generic depictions emphasize the connections between
this story and others like it. This storytelling technique offers the op-
posite of the unusual or the dramatic event. Here the seeming purpose of the story is to explore the typical or usual. Once again storytelling serves to get an ordinary life on the record and to understand.

"The Immigrant Story" ends with one of Paley's pared-down narratives: a one-page tale that includes years of living and dying. This
story about the hard times of his immigrant parents is told by Jack,
who uses it to explain his own anger and bad disposition. Through
Jack's oral tale, Paley reveals the uses we make of our family stories to
understand our own lives. Paley thought about this story for years
before she figured out how to tell it:

You look for the form and until you have the form, you can't tell the
story. And the form, I don't know how it's gotten; I consider it
received, like grace. How to tell the story. I have a story in my book
which I use as an example of that. It's called "The Immigrant Story."
Well, I knew that story for twenty-five years. I didn't know how to
tell it and I had to tell it not just in terms of the last paragraph which
said, his mother and father came from Poland, etc. but in terms of
everything that came after that which I had to put first. But I didn't
understand that. It took me, really, twenty years to figure out how to

tell that story so that it could be understood for what it was. That is not "new" . . . I don't think of that as "new." I just think of it as trying to tell a certain kind of story and not having the means. As far as I am concerned, the means did not exist in my literary education or in my experience so I had to wait until I had enough writing experience to be able to tell that story.[20]

Paley knows that she is inventing narrative structure in order to tell these stories. But the point is not novelty for its own sake; the point is to find a form that will accommodate her previously untold stories.

Later the Same Day

In her latest volume, Paley continues to work with extremely short stories. Four of the stories in *Later the Same Day* are complete in two pages or less. Three of these use the title to provide a context and interpretive frame for the story that follows. "In This Country But in Another Language, My Aunt Refuses to Marry the Men Everyone Wants Her To" appears in danger of having a title longer than the story itself. The story never mentions marriage after the title, but, narrated by the niece, it pursues the question of whether Sonia, the unmarried aunt, has had a life. The family's consensus is that she has not: "Sonia. One reason I don't close my eyes at night is I think about you. You know it. What will be? You have no life" (108). But the niece refuses to accept the family answer as the final judgment. Instead, she refers the question back to her aunt: "Sonia, tell me no or yes. Do you have a life?" "If you really want to know," her aunt tells her, "read Dostoevsky" (108). With this cryptic remark, Sonia emphasizes the importance of interior life over external event. The title of this piece carries the weight of exposition, instructing us in how to read the fragment that follows so that it opens out into a whole life.

In a similar way, "A Man Told Me the Story of His Life" and "This Is a Story about My Friend George, the Toy Inventor" provide valuable contexts for the tales that follow. "A Man Told Me" directs our attention to this story as a told tale, one that the writer simply records and thereby preserves. This context is reiterated in the opening words of the story: "Vicente said." "This Is a Story" recalls Paley's concern with writing from and to her friends, saving lives by telling their stories. The major point of this two-page story seems to be the presentation of George's redefinition of beauty as closely related to function—a discovery he makes by attempting unsuccessfully to improve on the design of the ordinary pinball machine. "This Is a Story" is only one very short step away from the types of stories one repeats at the end of the day to one's intimate friends or family members.

"Mother" is not a story according to conventional narrative structure, but more of a remembrance. The narrator begins with an expression of longing to once again see her mother "in the doorway" (111). She has heard a song on the radio voicing that sentiment and she recalls the various doorways where her mother once stood looking at her. In the daughter's memory, the mother seems to stand perpetually in doorways seeking connection with her daughter and her husband. This extremely brief story repeats its conclusion. The mother stands in the doorway talking to her daughter; their unsatisfactory communication is followed by the apparent conclusion, "Then she died." But the narrative continues with a recollection of the mother and father in the living room. Again, as with her daughter, the mother seeks unsuccessfully to engage her husband in conversation. The final sentence repeats the earlier conclusion, "Then she died." The structure is anything but linear. It can perhaps best be described as circular since it moves twice through the same cycle. We are left with the strong sense that these are two emblematic scenes that represent many similar ones. For each of her family members the opportunity to engage in communication with the mother is abruptly closed off with the finality of "Then she died" (112). Through this unconventional structure, "Mother" accomplishes a poignant expression of loss and laments a premature death without ever becoming sentimental. This story has none of the plot development associated with dominant narrative, yet once again with a few simple strokes it suggests an entire life.

In her most recent work Paley continues to probe the limits of genre and the relationship between orality and literature. The 1989 War Resisters League peace calendar, *365 Reasons Not to Have Another War,* features Paley's writing (both prose and poetry).[21] The format of the calendar favors brief entries, so longer stories necessarily are not included here. Nevertheless, it is interesting to find ten new prose pieces that could be considered short short stories. Two of these ("Answers I" and "Answers II") are only a half a page in length; the longest is a mere three pages. Although some of the stories make use of Paley's recurrent character Faith, others might easily be autobiography. In the introduction, Paley simply calls these works "prose pieces." Thus it is difficult in some cases to determine whether a particular piece is a short story or a memoir. The fact that one looks for either the names of recurrent characters or contextual evidence (grouping the works in a short story collection would be an example of such evidence) in an attempt to determine genre reveals just how far Paley has moved outside of conventional generic categories. She has stories to tell, and it makes no difference to her whether the stories are "real" or "imagined."

"Midrash on Happiness" is a particularly interesting example of how Paley continues to develop the short story. In rabbinic literature, midrash is "a genre of biblical exegesis" that "engages in ever-new revelations of an originary text."[22] These interpretations are often fanciful and remarkably open. Paley's midrash reports Faith's attempt to define happiness. The originary text in this case might well be understood as the dominant culture, which would never define happiness according to Paley's woman-centered terms. This project of definition is a complex one, for each definition is made up of dominant terms which must be redefined from Faith's muted perspective. The opening sentences of the story are typical: "What she meant by happiness, she said, was the following: she meant having (or having had) (or continuing to have) everything. By everything, she meant, first, the children, then a dear person to live with, preferably a man, but not necessarily, (by live with, she meant for a long time but not necessarily)."

This text is interesting not only because of the series of definitions, each one depending on yet another elaboration, but also because of its openness. This openness begins with the parenthetical phrases in the first sentence and continues in the second sentence with the qualifiers "preferably" and "but not necessarily." The text asserts a commitment to diversity even as it insists on a particular definition of happiness. It acknowledges that for some (possibly including Faith) "having had" everything might constitute happiness. And although we know from previous stories that Faith's ideal "dear person" is male, her use of the phrase "dear person" rather than "dear man," her inclusion of the word "preferably," and the emphasis on flexibility provided by the phrase "but not necessarily" all combine to open the text to lesbian readers as well as heterosexual women. (It is interesting to note that the first "but not necessarily" did not appear in an earlier draft of the story—thus, we have textual evidence of a move toward an increasingly more open and inclusive text.)[23]

Like certain longer Paley stories (for instance, "Friends" and "Ruthy and Edie"), this little two-and-a-half-page tale is constructed out of female talk. According to the terms of narrative convention, nothing happens. Faith explores the meaning of happiness as she walks through the city with her friend Ruth. Such walks "arm in arm with a woman friend" are one of the crucial components in her recipe for a happy life. Throughout most of the story, Ruth listens as Faith elaborates, but when she gives voice to her only real speech in this tale (excepting a one-line remark earlier), her comments locate the flaw in Faith's definition and the tension with which the story struggles. It is when Faith adds love to her recipe that Ruth demurs:

> Nowadays it [love and/or happiness] seems like pride, I mean overweening pride, when you look at the children and think we don't have time to do much (by time Ruth meant both her personal time and the planet's time). When I read in the papers and hear all this boom boom bellicosity, the guys out-daring each other, I see we have to change it all—the world—without killing it absolutely—without killing it, that'll be the trick the kids'll have to figure out. Until that begins, I don't understand happiness, what you mean by it.

Ruthy has located a problem that haunts the pages of Paley's fiction, the problem of personal happiness and personal solutions in a world poised on the brink of destruction. Faith, reminded of "public suffering," is ashamed. She explains to Ruthy, "I know all that. I do, but sometimes walking with a friend I forget the world." This story provides both an eloquent statement of the problem and an eloquent resolution. Though neither Paley nor her alter-ego Faith would condone personal life as a retreat from world responsibility, the care for the world they articulate proceeds from just the sort of fellow feeling that sometimes allows one in a moment of happiness to "forget the world."

The critics who complain that Paley's shortest stories lack development and fail to go anywhere are working out of a dominant tradition that defines what stories can be told. But Paley refuses to begin with the predetermined narrative structures of the literary tradition. Instead, she begins with what's hidden: "fiction or literature should really illuminate. I mean, art in general, painting, whatever—you pick up the rock and what's hidden should be seen and known."[24] Beginning with what she has called the dark lives of women, Paley draws on and extends a women's oral narrative tradition that ignores dominant concerns with dramatic conflict, point-making, and heroism in order to feature the emotional content of ordinary experience, celebrate the connections that unite people to one another, and memorialize and make sense of the events of everyday life. In the process, she not only reveals connections between women's orality and women's literacy, she also transforms the dominant narrative strategies that shape our beliefs about what stories can be told.

6
Voices from Who Knows Where

"I object not to facts but to people sitting in trees talking senselessly, voices from who knows where . . ."

—"A CONVERSATION WITH MY FATHER," *EC*, 162

W omen's storytelling styles (and communication styles in general) move away from the monologic styles of the male dominant standard toward a collaborative style that empowers multiple voices. An examination of narrative voice in Paley's stories reveals that in a similar way she has developed narrative strategies that challenge the monologic power of the narrator while promoting empathy and identification with the other.

The narrator is a powerful speaker, controlling our view of the story and shaping our perception of events. Like the public speaker, the narrator engages in what is primarily a one-way pattern of communication, without giving readers or other characters the opportunity to contribute to the telling of the story. But Paley's narrative voice manifests a growing resistance to the monologic power of the narrator. This resistance begins with a strategy used by many other twentieth-century writers, subjective narration. Paley extends the challenge to monologism available through subjective narration with four techniques: (1) she forges connections between the narrator and the reader through questions that invite readers to identify with the narrator's perspective; (2) she makes use of a first-person plural point of view that creates a collective narrator; (3) she incorporates perspectives of identification with the other into the narration; and (4) she includes in her collections stories that provide contradictory first-person accounts. But her most profound and original challenge to monologism is her use of what I call collaborative narration, a technique whereby narrators' versions of events are corrected and amended by the characters in the story. This chapter traces the development of Paley's resistance to monologic power by examining each of these challenges.

Subjective Narration

First-person narrators provide an obvious antidote to the objective, authoritative stance of the traditional "voice of God" narrator, a narrator who might well be regarded as one of the more oppressive voices in fiction. Because subjective narration is grounded in the perspective of a fictional character, the necessary human limitations of the narrator are more readily recognized by the reader, and the narrator's authority is mitigated.

Paley makes frequent and varied use of first-person narrators (in thirty-three of her forty-five published stories),[1] employing storytellers who range from childhood to old age, women and men, and members of diverse racial and ethnic groups.[2] This use of first-person narrators allows her to employ informal and intimate styles of discourse and to move away from the narrative objectivity and authority associated with more distanced and formal storytellers.[3]

For Paley, stories are created through the process of listening to the voice of the other. "I can't find my own way of speaking until I have other voices. It's almost other voices that give me the strength or the permission or whatever to go through with it." Fiction is a way of "trying to get the world to speak to you."[4] Each of the first three short stories she wrote is narrated in the first person by a speaker quite distinct from Paley herself. She describes the breakthrough that allowed her to begin hearing the other voices so crucial to her storytelling:

> You hear the expression "breakthrough," and it really was a breaking through. I had just been so distressed about—well, about the things I'm writing about: all these friendships and the guys upstairs and the women friends I was getting closer and closer to. And all of these problems: the way people live in this world and the relationships and . . . what it was all about—I just couldn't deal with it in poetry. I really had an awful lot of pressure. The first story I wrote, actually, was "The Contest." Because I was trying to figure out what made all these guys tick—this guy who was upstairs was the one really; I did

my best, I got into his head and I just sorta sat there and I said, "I've gotta write this story." And then the second one was "Goodbye and Good Luck."

And before I wrote those stories, I was just stuck in my own voice. Until I was able to use other people's voices, until I was able to hear other people's voices, that I'd been hearing all my life, you know, I was just talking me-me-me. While I was doing that, I couldn't write these stories. And when I was able to get into other voices consciously, or use what I was hearing, and become the story hearer—when I could do that, I just suddenly wrote them. It was a true breakthrough.[5]

"The Contest" offers a good example of the way first-person narration not only allows a speaker to speak for himself but also reveals the narrator's personal limitations. Freddy, the narrator, is a young man determined to avoid marriage and commitment at all costs. He reveals his cavalier attitude toward women in his description of Dotty Wasserman, the girlfriend who attempts unsuccessfully to secure a marriage proposal from this fellow:

> My last girl was Jewish, which is often a warm kind of girl, concerned about food intake and employability. They don't like you to work too hard, I understand, until you're hooked and then, you bastard, sweat!
>
> A medium girl, size twelve, a clay pot with handles—she could be grasped. (*DM*, 67)

Paley explains that when she wrote this story she "was thinking about women and what was wrong between men and women and I thought, 'why not see how a man thinks on this issue?' so I let him do the talking." Agreeing with her interviewer that she was "still rough on him [despite letting him do the talking]," Paley elaborates: "I let him talk his own language, and let him say exactly what he wanted to say. And I've had men come up to me and say, 'That was great! You really understand him. He really let that bitch have it!'"[6] Paley's experience with "The Contest" illustrates the capacity of first-person narration to simultaneously respect each person's story and reveal (at least to sensitive readers) the limitations of any single story.

But subjective narrators, even those whose bias is obvious, still retain the power of the monologue and the capacity to define a world of self and other based on difference. Yet Paley's fiction is marked by an impulse toward identification that has led her in a progression away from the subjectivity and solipsism of the first-person narrator toward an ever greater empowerment of multiple voices.

Connecting the Narrator and the Reader

Although first-person narrators frequently speak in confidential and intimate tones, Paley's narrators seem to do so to a greater extent than most. Her narrators regularly speak as if to a peer, and the reader comes to feel included in the text in a singularly familiar way. This is girl talk (or nowadays, perhaps, woman talk), the sort of intimate sharing that occurs between close female friends around the kitchen table. Faith describes such a tone in "The Long-Distance Runner" when she speaks of her desire to "talk lovingly like sisters" with Mrs. Luddy.

Paley effects this tone in part through the use of questions that directly invite the reader/listener to share in the judgments of the narrator. In the preceding chapter we noted the prevalence of a collaborative style of storytelling among women. The tendency toward a male preference for monologue and a female preference for cooperative speech styles has been noted by a variety of researchers.[7] Paley's narrators make regular appeals to the reader/listener to share their opinions or conclusions. In this way, the reader is constructed as a peer and encouraged to take a participatory stance.

The first instance of this technique occurs in "A Woman, Young and Old." The thirteen-year-old narrator, Josephine, is offered a sip of beer by her grandmother: "And Josie dear, it's awful warm out and your mama won't mind. You're nearly a young lady. Would you like a sip of icy beer?" Josephine's narrative question takes it for granted that the reader will share her response: "Wasn't that respectful?" she asks us (*DM,* 28). Such a question simultaneously requests and assumes agreement.

Examples of this technique occur with greater frequency in Paley's second volume. In "Distance," Mrs. Raftery describes how young people relate to older people, and her assertion concludes with a similar appeal to the reader for agreement: "I've noticed it. All of a sudden they look at you, and then it comes to them, young people, they are bound to outlast you, so they temper up their icy steel and stare into about an inch away from you a lot. Have you noticed it?" (*EC*, 22–23). Mrs. Raftery's question does more than invite the reader to share her perspective; it assumes a common experience and thus posits a reader who is close to her in age. She addresses someone who may not have noticed this phenomenon yet but who has had occasion to do so.

Faith, the chatty narrator of "Faith in a Tree," regularly appeals to the reader and invites us into the text. Explaining that her one moment of fame occurred because she was "the third commercial airflight baby passenger in the entire world," she asks a series of questions that encourage the reader to examine this event from her point of view: "*Why* would anyone send a little baby anywhere alone? What was my mother trying to prove? That I was independent? That she wasn't the sort to hang on? That in the sensible, socialist, Zionist world of the future, she wouldn't cry at my wedding? 'You're an American child. Free. Independent.' Now what does that mean?" (*EC*, 80).

This technique is not limited to female narrators. The male storyteller of "The Little Girl" asks, "But wasn't it a shame, them two studs. Why they take it out on her?" (*EC*, 157). The first statement in particular invites the reader to agree with the narrator's evaluation.

In "The Long-Distance Runner," Faith asks a tag question, a variety of question that some research suggests is more prevalent among female speakers.[8] "All creation is secret, isn't that true?" (*EC*, 179). Such a question manifests a concern with the listener's reaction and a reluctance to take an isolated position. When such questions occur in actual conversations, they also elicit some sort of a reaction, even if only a minimal nod of the head.

Questions for the reader continue to be important in Paley's latest volume. In a passage quoted in chapter 1, the narrator asks "Don't you wish you could rise powerfully above your time and name? I'm sure we all try . . ." ("The Story Hearer," *LD*, 140). Here the way such questions function to connect narrator and reader is made explicit by the "we" of the text. In another particularly telling example, Faith reports that Jack "called the store to tell the salesmen not to sell too many kitchen sets without him, he couldn't afford to give away all that commission" and asks, "Wouldn't you think that would annoy the men?" She then explains, "Jack says I don't understand the way men talk to one another" ("Listening," *LD,* 206). What makes this example especially interesting is that it not only invites the reader into a shared intimacy with the narrator but assumes that the reader is female.

What all of these examples illustrate is the extent to which Paley's storytellers invite the reader into the text, taking as given a set of common assumptions and experiences. Such a strategy facilitates the move beyond a muted state by assuming sympathetic and congenial story hearers. Indeed, in *Later the Same Day* it is not unusual to find explicit evidence that Paley is in the process of constructing a "we" that includes speaker and listener. Narrators address readers with such inclusive phrases as "because you know" (144), "as we know" (121), and "all of us know" (200). The assumption of a common body of knowledge facilitates the creation of a common language and undermines the monologic power of a single narrator.

Collective Narration

In addition to inviting the reader into a participatory relationship with the storyteller, Paley's most recent work has begun to employ another strategy that challenges the narrator's monologic authority. Three of her stories rely on a first-person plural point of view that provides a sort of collective narration. *Enormous Changes* offers the first glimpse of this technique. In "Politics," the initial sentence states that "A group of mothers from our neighborhood went downtown to the Board of Estimate Hearing and sang a song" (139). But in this instance, the first-person plural occurs only in the introduction, providing a communal context for the remainder of the story, which is told from a third-person point of view.

The first full-blown instance of this technique appears in "Somewhere Else." Faith narrates this story, announcing in the first paragraph that "Twenty-two Americans were touring China. I was one of them" (*LD,* 47). Although she begins in the singular, throughout much of her tale she uses the pronoun "we," a "we" that includes the group of touring Americans, but often more specifically includes Faith and her two friends Ruth and Ann. One passage illustrates with particular clarity that Faith, Ruth, and Ann are the most important part of Faith's "we": "Now he shouldn't have said that. It made us stop listening—especially Ruth Larsen, Ann Reyer, and me" (48).

As the story unfolds, the connections between these women and the similarity of their viewpoints become clear. Faith, Ruth, and Ann share common friendships, politics, social class, age, and sex. The "we" of Faith's narration illustrates their collective identity in this story.

"Friends" again makes a "we" of Faith and her friends. This time Faith, Ann, and Susan have gone to visit their dying friend Selena. From the opening sentence ("To put us at our ease, to quiet our hearts as she lay dying, our dear friend Selena . . ."), these women function as a collective narrator, united in sympathy and understanding. Although Faith actually tells the tale, she speaks for the group. In an interview with Paley, Joan Lidoff observes that "Friends" seems to have a kind of collective heroine and relates this to psychological theories suggesting that "women may continue to think of themselves more collectively, more in connection with other people, than as distinctly separate individuals." Paley responds with a description of the kinds of bonds between her and her friends that inspired the story: "In that story 'Friends' those women, we *were* awfully close and we began by hanging out in the park together, but we did an awful lot of politics together. We really did have a collective existence in a way, you know."[9] Paley's comment explicitly acknowledges the link between collective narration and a species of collective existence common to women.

The final example of collective narration is "This Is for My Friend George, the Toy Inventor." The singular first-person of the title is the only singular first-person in the story's narration. Even when the narrator reports her own speech, she speaks as part of a group: "When we saw it, we said, George! This is not a pinball machine alone. This is the poem of a pinball machine, the essence made delicately concrete, and so forth" (147). One is tempted to note that these are collective sayings we doubt ever got said. The "and so forth" supports the conclusion that each of the members of this "we" made comments of this sort rather than all speaking these particular words in unison. But the salient point here is that Paley has again given us a narrative speaker who is not Faith alone or even Grace alone, but Faith and/or Grace and friends. These women have so much collective life that at times they speak in a collective voice. When they do so, they speak outside a dominant monologic tradition in a voice that resists the monologue's power to define.

Identification with the Other

A third technique Paley has developed for breaking down the monologic (and potentially solipsistic) power of the first-person narrator is
the use of first-person narrators who interject a perspective of identification with the other into their accounts. In "Goodbye and Good
Luck," when Rosie plans to move out on her own so her lover can
visit her, her mother responds, "You! You, a nothing, a rotten hole in
a piece of cheese, are you telling me what is life!" Rosie as storyteller
identifies the source of this remark:

> Very insulted, I went away from her. But I am good-natured—you
> know fat people are like that—kind, and I thought to myself, poor
> Mama . . . it is true she got more of an idea of life than me. She
> married who she didn't like, a sick man, his spirit already swallowed
> up by God. He never washed. He had an unhappy smell. His teeth
> fell out, his hair disappeared, he got smaller, shriveled up little by
> little, till goodbye and good luck he was gone and only came to
> Mama's mind when she went to the mailbox under the stairs to get
> the electric bill. (*LD*, 13)

Despite her mother's insult, Rosie manages to empathize with the
mother's circumstances and create a context in which the mother's
harsh words become understandable. Rosie performs a similar maneuver when describing a subsequent visit with her mother: "So I
went and stayed with Mama for a week's vacation and cleaned up all
the closets and scrubbed the walls till the paint came off. She was
very grateful, all the same her hard life made her say, 'Now we see the
end. If you live like a bum, you are finally a lunatic'" (15). Again,
Rosie manages through reference to her mother's difficult life to construct a rationale that partially justifies these harsh words.

In "An Interest in Life," Virginia, a welfare mother whose husband has deserted her, gets solace from the weekly visits of her old
friend John. But eventually his visits grow infrequent: "I tried looking at it from his man point of view, and I thought he has to take a
bus, the tubes, and a subway to see me; and then the subway, the
tubes, and a bus to go back home at 1 A.M. It wouldn't be any trouble
at all for him to part with us forever" (98). Here the narrator explicitly identifies her shift in point of view ("his man point of view")—a
shift this phrase links to gender differences—before giving an account of John's behavior that is at odds with her own self-interest.

In "Gloomy Tune," a first-person narrator supports and identifies with another character: "One day . . . Chuchi Gomez slipped in an olive-oil puddle left by a lady whose bottle broke. She picked up the bottle pieces, but didn't do a thing about the oil. I wouldn't know what to do about the oil either" (*EC*, 55). "She . . . didn't do a thing about the oil" has the construction of an accusation, encouraging the reader to conclude that this woman has behaved negligently, but the next statement, "I wouldn't know what to do about the oil either," supports her behavior and invites us to identify with her predicament.

When the institutionalized only daughter of white, Jewish, and racist Zagrowsky becomes pregnant by the African American gardener at the mental institution, Zagrowsky invents this explanation for her behavior: "I could imagine what happened. Cissy always loved flowers. When she was a little girl she was planting seeds every minute and sitting all day in front of the flower pot to see the little flower cracking up the seed. So she must have watched him and watched him. He dug up the earth. He put in the seed. She watches" ("Zagrowsky Tells," 168). Where we might have expected fury from Zagrowsky at a daughter who has violated several of his cherished beliefs, we find instead a tender explanation of what drew her to behave as she did.

In "Listening," Faith, while distributing leaflets calling for the United States to honor the Geneva agreements, encounters "a young man in uniform, a soldier":

> I thought, when he leaves or if I leave first, I'll give him a leaflet. I don't want to but I will. Then I thought, Poor young fellow, God knows what his experience has been; his heart, if it knew, would certainly honor the Geneva Agreements, but it would probably hurt his feelings to hear one more word about how the U.S.A. is wrong again and how he is an innocent instrument of evil. He would take it personally, although we who are mothers and have been sweethearts—all of us know that "soldier" is what a million boys have been forced to be in every single one of a hundred generations. ("Listening," 200)

In all of these examples, the first-person narrator brings us closer to the imagined perspective of one of the other characters. Paley's narrators, through an act of identification, repeatedly imagine reasons for the apparently unreasonable or unsympathetic behavior of characters in the stories they tell.

Contradictory First-Person Accounts

Throughout Paley's three volumes of short stories, certain characters (primarily Faith, her family, and her friends) recur. This core of connected stories makes up nearly half of Paley's published stories.[10] In conjunction with this use of recurrent characters and situations, Paley has developed a fourth strategy for subverting the monologic power of the first-person narrator. She sometimes allows a different first-person narrator to give us an alternative perspective on events or individuals we have earlier seen from another viewpoint.

For instance, in "An Interest in Life," Virginia, commenting on Mrs. Raftery, the mother of her married lover, tells us:

> Mrs. Raftery is sometimes silly and sick from her private source of cheap wine. She expects John often. "Honor your mother, what's the matter with you, John?" she complains. "Honor. Honor."
>
> "Virginia dear," she says. "You never would've taken John away to Jersey like Margaret. I wish he'd've married you."
>
> "You didn't like me much in those days." "That's a lie," she says. I know she's a hypocrite, but no more than the rest of us. (*DM*, 99–100)

When Mrs. Raftery speaks for herself in "Distances," a more sympathetic portrait emerges: "I wait on the stoop steps to see John on summer nights, as he hasn't enough time to visit me and Ginny both, and I need the sight of him, though I don't know why. I like the street anyway, and the hot night when the ice-cream truck brings all the dirty kids and the big nifty boys with their hunting-around eyes. I put a touch of burgundy on my strawberry ice-cream cone as my father said we could on Sunday, which drives these sozzle-headed ladies up the brown brick wall, so help me Mary" (*EC*, 26). Asked about the relationship between the two stories, Paley explains, "I felt I hadn't done justice to the old woman. And I was sort of curious about her."[11] In Virginia's story, Mrs. Raftery is a nosy, judgmental, outspoken wine-guzzler (although not without kindhearted impulses) while in Mrs. Raftery's version of events, Virginia is the scandal of the neighborhood ("tell me, young man, how you'll feel married to a girl that every wild boy on the block has been leaning his thumbs on her titties like she was a Carvel dairy counter, tell me that?"). But when we hear their own accounts of their behavior, a much more sympathetic view prevails. Together, the stories make the point that almost any set of behaviors can make sense when viewed from the inside.

Similarly, Faith, a frequent narrator of Paley's stories, emerges in her own accounts as a highly reliable and sympathetic speaker. In fact, her values and experiences have so much in common with the implied author of these works that critics regularly equate her with Paley. But in "Zagrowsky Tells," we get a rare external view of Faith from a first-person narrator who does not find her so sympathetic. To Zagrowsky, Faith is "a woman minus a smile," who gives him "a look like God in judgment" (*LD*, 151). When Faith hears the story of how Zagrowsky, whose pharmacy Faith and her friends had picketed years before for its racist practices, has come to have an African American grandchild, she immediately begins to advise him to seek out a more integrated neighborhood for the benefit of the child. Zagrowsky responds:

> Listen, Miss, Miss Faith—do me a favor, don't teach me.
>   I'm not teaching you Iz, its just . . .
>   Don't answer me every time I say something. Talking talking. It's true. What for? To whom? Why? Nettie's right. It's our business. She's telling me Emmanuel's life.
>   You don't know nothing about it, I yell at her. Go make a picket line. Don't teach me. (172)

Seen suddenly through Zagrowsky's eyes, Faith appears insensitive and patronizing.

Paley has commented on how important it is that Zagrowsky tell his own story. When she first tried to tell his story, she couldn't get beyond the first two paragraphs for about two years: "I was stuck. I couldn't figure it out. And the reason was I was having [Faith] tell it. She was going to tell the story to Jack. . . . At a certain point I realized that she didn't know the first damn thing about him. He was the only one who knew. . . . He was supposed to tell that story." [12]

Zagrowsky tells his story because "the lungs are for breathing, not secrets. . . . if you want to breathe, you got to tell." Faith responds with judgment and advice. That the character so corrected is closely identified with the voice of the author only makes the implicit message about the difficulty of really listening to the other all the more powerful.

Collaborative Narration

Although all of these strategies undermine monologic power, Paley, during the course of her career, has developed ever greater challenges to the authority of a single narrator controlling the story. She has done this by empowering characters to interrupt, correct, and contribute to the narrator's tale.

In her first volume, we can see the unrealized impulse for this type of dialogue. In "An Interest in Life," John admits to Virginia that he had wanted to marry her years earlier. This leads Virginia to a narrative digression of several paragraphs as she speaks of the husband who has deserted her. She tells the reader, "I didn't tell John, but the truth is, I would never have married him. Once I met my husband with his winking looks, he was my only interest. Wild as I had been with John and others, I turned all my wildness over to him and then there was no question in my mind." Her explanation continues, as she apparently addresses the reader in narrative time. But when John speaks, there is a strong implication that her thoughts have occurred in story time and that John is responding to her narrative digression: "'A funny guy,' said John, guessing where my thoughts had gone" (*DM*, 93–94).

A similar instance occurs in the final story in *The Little Disturbances of Man*. The narrator offers the reader this comment on her friend:

> The organization of his ideas was all wrong; I was drawn to the memory of myself—a mere stripling of a girl—the day I learned that the shortest distance between two points is a great circle.
>
> "Anyway, you ought to think in shorter sentences," he suggested, although I hadn't said a word. Old Richard-the-Liver-Headed, he saw right through to the heart of the matter, my syntax. ("The Floating Truth," 178–179)

In both these instances, a comment on the narrative comes from a character in story time, but this unusual occurrence is naturalized by suggesting that the character was somehow following the narrator's thoughts.

In her second volume, Paley takes this technique a step farther. In "Faith in the Afternoon," a third-person narrator reflects Faith's consciousness:

> Faith is perfectly willing to say it herself, to any good listener: she loved Ricardo. She began indeed to love herself, to love the prop- erties which, for a couple of years anyway, extracted such heart- warming activity from him.
>
> Well, Faith argues whenever someone says, "Oh really, Faithy, what do you mean—love?" She must have loved Ricardo. She had two boys with him. (*EC*, 35)

Here the dialogue between Faith's narration of her own life and the competing perspective on it that a friend might offer are included through the use of a third-person narrator who both reflects Faith's thoughts and reports the questions of a possible other. The dialogue between competing points of view is now explicit in the text, but the presence of a reflector narrator preserves narrative conventions.

But with the story "Faith in a Tree," Paley abandons efforts to fol- low conventional distinctions between story time and narrative time, and allows a free-wheeling exchange to occur that breaks down boundaries between narrator and characters and openly comments on the narrator's version of events. Faith is at the neighborhood park with her children, Richard and Anthony, where she sits in a sycamore tree and discourses on whatever subject chances to come to mind. She begins the story by letting us know this is not where she wants to be: "Just when I most needed important conversation, a sniff of the man-wide world, that is, at least one brainy companion who could translate my friendly language into his tongue of undying car- nal love, I was forced to lounge in our neighborhood park, sur- rounded by children" (*EC*, 77). The opening five pages of the story consist almost entirely of Faith's narration as she reports her thoughts and observations on all she surveys. When she is eventually ad- dressed and enters into conversation with the other characters, her remarks in story time are indicated by quotation marks. But when

Richard responds jealously to Faith's admiration of another child, we get the following exchange:

> "We're really a problem to you, Faith, we keep you not free," Richard says. "Anyway, it's true you're crazy about anyone but us."
>
> It's true I do like the other kids. I am not too cool to say Alex's Sharon really is a peach. But you, you stupid kid, Richard! Who could match me for pride or you for brilliance? Which one of the smart third-grade kids in a class of learned Jews, Presbyterians, and bohemians? You are one of the two smartest and the other one is Chinese—Arnold Lee, who does make Richard look a little simple, I admit it. But did you ever hear of a child who, when asked to write a sentence for the word "who" (they were up to the hard *wh*'s), wrote and then magnificently, with Oriental lisp, read the following: "Friend, tell me WHO among the Shanghai merchants does the largest trade?"
>
> "That's a typical yak yak out of you, Faith," says Richard. (84)

The preceding pattern of using quotation marks to indicate direct address leads the reader to assume that Faith's statement, even though it contains direct address to Richard, reports her thoughts rather than anything spoken in story time. The third-person reference to Richard in the middle of her speech seems to confirm this conclusion, as does the question directly addressing the reader ("did you ever hear of a kid who"). But Richard's response startles the reader with its implication that he has had access to this apparently narrative passage. The ambiguous status of this passage is compounded in the next paragraph when Paley makes another statement, clearly addressed to Richard ("Now Richard, listen to me") that *is* enclosed in quotation marks.

From this point, the status of the narrative passages is frequently called into question. In response to one of Richard's smart remarks, Faith asks, without quotes, "How can you answer that boy?" This appears to be an aside addressed to the reader, but it is followed by a reply from one of the park mothers: "'You don't,' says Mrs. Junius Finn, glad to say a few words" (84–85).

When Faith's friend Kitty directs her attention to a handsome man in the park, Faith invents a complicated explanation for his presence. The absence of quotes makes it difficult to determine whether

the passage is one of indirect discourse, reporting an exchange between Kitty and Faith, or simply Faith's private speculations. Kitty's
quoted comment, "Don't even think like that," does little to clarify
the situation.

Two music lovers walk past, their heads bent to their transistor,
and are heard to remark, "Jack, do you hear what I hear?" "Damnit
yes, the over-romanticizing and the under-Baching, I can't believe
it." Faith comments:

> Well, I must say when darkness covers the earth and great
> darkness the people, I will think of you: two men with smart ears. I
> don't believe civilization can do a lot more than educate a person's
> senses. If it's truth and honor you want to refine, I think the Jews
> have some insight. Make no images, imitate no God. After all, in
> His field, the graphic arts, He is pre-eminent. Then let that One who
> made the tan deserts and the blue Van Allen belt and the green
> mountains of New England be in charge of Beauty, which He ob-
> viously understands, and let man, who was full of forgiveness at Je-
> rusalem, and full of survival at Troy, let man be in charge of Good.
>
> "Faith, will you quit with your all-the-time philosophies," says
> Richard, my first- and disapproving-born. (89)

Once again, a passage that appears to be narrative has been heard and
commented on by Richard.

For the first time in her fiction, Paley has found a way to create a
collaborative narration, with characters entering into and commenting on the narrative passages. The result is exhilarating if sometimes a
bit confusing. In "A Conversation with My Father," Paley allows the
father to articulate the response of a conventionally trained reader to
this story: "I object not to facts but to people sitting in trees talking
senselessly, voices from who knows where . . ." (162).

It is interesting to note that the story in which Paley first finds the
freedom to give her characters the opportunity to comment on narrative passages finds the protagonist suspended above the earth in a
sycamore tree. No longer earth-bound, Faith is also liberated from
narrative convention. Her superhuman status in this story is further
indicated at the beginning of the text by a comparison between
God's celestial view of New York City and her own bird's-eye view.

Paley returns to this technique of collaborative narration in a second story in *Enormous Changes,* this time giving a character the opportunity to contradict the narrator. In "The Immigrant Story," Jack and the narrator (probably Faith) are fighting. Jack accuses Faith of having "a rotten rosy temperament. You were like that in sixth grade. One day you brought three American flags to school." Although no quotation marks are used in this story, Faith's response appears to be a narrative explanation: "That was true. I made an announcement to the sixth-grade assembly thirty years ago. I said: I thank God every day that I'm not in Europe. I thank God I'm American-born and live on East 172nd Street where there is a grocery store, a candy store, and a drugstore on one corner and on the same block a shul and two doctors' offices." The use of past tense, "That *was* true," and the inclusion of information that Jack apparently already knows, leaves the reader no doubt that this is a narrative passage. Thus Jack's response is a surprise: "One Hundred and Seventy-second Street was a pile of shit, he said. Everyone was on relief except you. Thirty people had t.b. Citizens and noncitizens alike starving until the war" (173). Jack contradicts a statement the narrator has made in narrative time (which according to narrative convention he has no access to) and then the two continue with their argument in story time.[13] Paley has thus devised an ingenious technique for reminding the reader that any narrator's version of a story is fallible and limited. Not content to inscribe multiple voices in the text through conventional narrative techniques, Paley subverts narrative control through a style of collaborative narration that even permits absolute contradictions.

Paley's most recent writing shows a continued and increasing willingness to experiment with collaborative narration. Her move away from the use of quotation marks adds to the ambiguity regarding speech that exists as narrative and speech that occurs in story time (scene). For example, in "Love," the narrator's husband claims to have had an affair with Dotty Wasserman, a character from an earlier Paley story. The narrator, who seems to be Paley herself, points out that this is impossible since Dotty is "a character in a book. She's not even a person." She demands to know, "What's this baloney about you and Dotty Wasserman?":

Nothing much. She was this crazy kid who hung around the bars. But she didn't drink. Really it was for the men, you know. Neither did I—drink too much, I mean. I was just hoping to get laid once in a while or maybe meet someone and fall madly in love.

He is that romantic. Sometimes I wonder if loving me in this homey life in middle age with two sets of bedroom slippers, one a skin of sandal for summer and the other pair lined with cozy sheepskin. It must be a disappointing experience for him.

He made a polite bridge over my conjectures. He said, She was also this funny mother in the park, years later, when we were all doing that municipal politics and I was married to Josephine. (*LD*, 4–5)

By describing the husband's second comment as a polite bridge over her conjectures, the narrator implies that her narrative passage was available to him. In "Dreamer in a Dead Language," the reflector-narrator says of Faith:

His voice had a timbre which reminded her of evening, maybe night-time. She had often thought of the way wide air lives and moves in a man's chest. Then it's strummed into shape by the short-stringed voice box to become a wonderful secondary sexual characteristic.

Your voice reminds me of evening too, said Philip. (*LD*, 12)

Examples of collaborative narration abound in "Friends," in which the relationship between narration and direct discourse is often ambiguous. For instance: "Susan's eyes opened. The death or dying of someone near or dear often makes people irritable, she stated. (She's been taking a course in relationships *and* interrelationships.) The real name of my seminar is Skills: Personal Friendship and Community. It's a very good course despite your snide remarks" (*LD*, 82).

Issues regarding time and place of speaking concern Paley less and less as she develops as a writer. At times, it almost seems as if the characters exist inside the head of the narrator, who knows them well enough to voice their objections to her story even when they are not present. At other times, it is as if the characters and narrator can both move freely between narrative and story time. Or perhaps, more accurately, Paley simply cannot be bothered with narrative conventions that get in the way of the stories she wants to tell. The stories she wants to tell are based on a firm belief that no one person has the corner on the truth. The truth can begin to emerge only when we learn to really listen to each other and when all are empowered to be both storytellers and story hearers.

Cassie's Challenge

Paley's strongest critique of the dangers inherent in monologic narration occurs in "Listening," the final story in her latest collection. The story is constructed, as the title suggests, around the experience of listening (see chapter 4 for a discussion of the associative pattern of organization in this story). In the opening scene, Faith overhears two conversations in a restaurant. Later, Jack and Faith talk about her late-middle-age desire to have another baby: "Now listen to me, he said. And we began to address each other slowly and formally as people often do when seriousness impedes ease; some stately dance is required. Listen. Listen, he said. Our old children are just about grown. Why do you want a new child? Haven't we agreed often, haven't we said that it had become noticeable that life is short and sorrowful?" (*LD*, 203–204). Later Richard appears on the scene, known, Faith tells us, "far and wide for his nosy ear." He wants to know, "what is this crap, Mother, this life is short and terrible. What is this metaphysical shit, what is this disease you intelligentsia are always talking about" (206). It is not until the final scene, however, that the significance of this focus on listening is crystallized for the reader.

Faith is driving down Broadway when she notices "a man in the absolute prime of life" crossing the street. She calls him to the attention of her friend Cassie, and a pivotal scene follows:

> He's nice, isn't he? I said to my friend Cassie.
>
> I suppose so, she said, but Faith, what is he, just a bourgeois on his way home.
>
> To everyday life, I said sighing with a mild homesickness.
>
> To whose everyday life, she said, goddamnit, whose?
>
> She turned to me, which is hard to do when you're strapped and stuffed into a bucket seat. Listen, Faith, why don't you tell my story? You've told everybody's story but mine. I don't even mean my whole story, that's my job. You probably can't. But I mean you've just omitted me from the other stories and I was there. In the restaurant and the train, right there. Where is Cassie? Where is *my* life? It's

been women and men, women and men, fucking, fucking. God-
damnit, where the hell is my woman and woman, woman-loving life
in all this? And it's not even sensible, because we *are* friends, we
work together, you even care about me at least as much as you do
Ruthy and Louise and Ann. You let them in all the time; it's really
strange, why have you left me out of everybody's life?

I took a deep breath and turned the car to the curb. I couldn't
drive. We sat there for about twenty minutes. Every now and then
I'd say, My God! or, Christ Almighty! neither of whom I usually call
on, but she was stern and wouldn't speak. Cassie, I finally said, I
don't understand it either; it's true, though, I know what you mean.
It must feel for you like a great absence of yourself. How could I
allow it. But it's not me alone, it's them too. I waited for her to say
something. Oh, but it *is* my fault. Oh, but why did you wait so
long? How can you forgive me?

Forgive you? She laughed. But she reached across the clutch.
With her hand she turned my face to her so my eyes would look into
her eyes. You are my friend, I know that, Faith, but I promise you, I
won't forgive you, she said. From now on, I'll watch you like a
hawk. I do not forgive you. (209–211)

Faith's omission is more blatant than simply ignoring the stories that
involve Cassie; she has written them while denying the presence of
her lesbian friend. The restaurant and the train are specific settings
from previous Paley stories; Ruthy, Louise, and Ann are recognizable Paley characters.[14] Cassie acknowledges that she is the only one
who can tell her whole story ("that's my job"), but she is angry with
her friend Faith for omitting her from the stories in which their lives
intersect.

Faith understands immediately what she has done. "A great absence of yourself" is what all marginalized peoples have encountered
when looking for their reflection in the pages of literature. But like
many of us, when confronted with the charge that she has failed as a
listener, she tries to shift some of the blame to society: "But it's not
me alone, it's them too." Cassie refuses to grace that excuse with a
reply. At last Faith accepts full responsibility for her sin of omission
and asks Cassie's forgiveness. But Cassie makes it clear that forgiveness is not possible. From now on, Faith must tell her stories

with the knowledge that Cassie, her unforgiving friend, is watching her "like a hawk."

This passage stands as a critique not only of the stories narrated by Faith but of Paley's entire corpus. Paley has worked at creating a literature of connection and inclusion, cutting across lines of class, race, religion, gender, and age to produce stories remarkable for their explicit attention to the multiple and diverse voices that must be heard from if we are to escape the dangers of solipsism. Yet none of her preceding forty-four stories has included a lesbian character, a fact that is the more striking when one considers that the stories are set in Greenwich Village and focus on the lives of women, many of whom are unconventional in one respect or another. Thus Paley indicts herself for her own failure as a listener. Paley has said of this story:

> I was working on that story, and I came to a point where I didn't know what to do next. I had already known it was about listening. I sort of knew that because it began with hearing those stories in the beginning of those guys talking. It began with thinking about telling stories, like he [Jack] says, why don't you tell me women's stories? and she says, Forget it. So it's really about listening. Then Richard overhears her and comes into the room and says, I heard you talking about all this metaphysical shit. It's all about listening. I didn't know what the heck to do, and then it suddenly really came to me. I'm such a big-shot about listening, but here I've been living/working with all these women who are as close to me . . . they're my real pals, I teach with a couple of them. And I've worked with them in the last ten years, you know in politics and women's Pentagon Action and different actions. And here I'm such a big-shot listener, and I haven't been listening! . . . I've heard it, but I didn't listen. You hear, but listening is another matter. So it suddenly came to me, that's what the story is about.[15]

Paley's articulation of the implication of this passage is clear and to the point. Her unrelenting insistence on listening includes even her own work in its critique and moves her toward an increasingly demanding politics of inclusion.

Cassie serves notice to all of Paley's readers that no narrator, not even the most politically sensitive, aware, and sympathetic, is immune to the danger of excluding voices different from her own. If Cassie could be written out of these stories, then other deletions and distortions must remain.

Cassie's challenge to Faith also represents the ultimate empowerment of characters to challenge the narrator's control of the story. Through a progressive development of narrative strategies that foster connection and inclusion, Paley dismantles the power of the narrator and moves narrator and characters to a more egalitarian relationship. As characters find their voices as storytellers, narrators must relinquish some of their monologic power. The result is a collaborative narration with the potential for expressing multiple and conflicting points of view. Paley seeks internal, intimate views of her characters, but never at the expense of any of the richly various voices that constitute her story world.

Conclusion

The Cassie scene is the culmination of a technique Paley has developed throughout her corpus. Faith is the character in Paley's fiction who seems closest to the author's own voice. Her values and viewpoint are, for the most part, strongly supported by the text. Yet in the final story of her second volume, "The Long-Distance Runner," Paley gives Faith the opportunity to recognize her own oblivion to white privilege; in "Zagrowsky Tells," Paley reveals Faith's tendency to smug self-righteousness; and now with Cassie, Faith confronts her own limitations as a listener and storyteller. It cannot be coincidental that "The Long-Distance Runner" concludes *Enormous Changes* and "Listening" concludes *Later the Same Day,* for both of these stories serve as an ultimate critique of the narrator's limitations.

At the level of both semantics and narrative structure, Paley writes a subversive text, a text that exists in dialogue with the monologic impulses of dominant literature. She is an artist dedicated to making language speak the untold stories of women, even when that means flouting the semantic and narrative conventions that construct women's silence. Paley's standard for an open and polyvocal text is a demanding one, so demanding that she herself fails to fully satisfy it. That very failure becomes a profound critique of the capacity of literary discourse to mute the voice of the other. Even the most well-intentioned listener, Paley reminds us, is prone to suppress voices of difference. Only the most demanding politics of inclusion, one un-afraid to turn the critique of monologism on the self, can begin to create the sort of open discourse that will allow everyone to find a voice. Even then Paley would not be satisfied, for she recognizes that a truly polyvocal literature depends not only on texts that open up to many voices but on many voices creating the tales. As Cassie recog-nizes, anyone who wants her whole story told must tell it herself.

Notes

Introduction

1. Jacqueline Taylor, "Grace Paley on Storytelling and Story Hearing," *Literature in Performance* 7 (1987): 52.

2. Joan Lidoff, "Clearing Her Throat: An Interview with Grace Paley," *Shenandoah* 32, no. 3 (1981): 7.

3. Kay Bonetti, *American Audio Prose Library Presents an Interview with Grace Paley.*

4. Karen Endor and Naomi Thiers, "We're Talking with Each Other More and More: An Interview with Grace Paley," *Off Our Backs* 18 (April 1988): 4.

5. Quotations from Paley's stories will be cited parenthetically using the following abbreviations: *The Little Disturbances of Man: DM; Enormous Changes at the Last Minute: EC; Later the Same Day: LD.*

6. Grace Paley, "Introduction to 'A Conversation with My Father,'" in *Fathers: Reflections by Daughters,* ed. Ursula Owen, 233.

7. William Novak, "The Uses of Fiction: To Reveal and to Heal," *America,* June 8, 1974, 459–460; and Jonathan Baumback, "Life-Size," *Partisan Review* 42, no. 2 (1975): 303–304.

8. Paley, "Introduction," 233.

9. Kathleen Hulley, "Introduction: Grace Paley's Resistant Form," *Delta, revue du Centre d'Étude et de Recherches sur les Écrivains du Sud aux États-Unis* 14 (1982): 9–10.

10. Kathleen Hulley, "Interview with Grace Paley," *Delta, revue du Centre d'Étude et de Recherches sur les Écrivains du Sud aux États-Unis* 14 (1982): 27.

11. Ibid., 33.

12. Dale Spender provides a comprehensive book-length treatment of this topic. With respect to the so-called generic use of *he,* for instance, she notes that in 1746 John Kirkby invented "Eighty Eight Grammatical Rules"

and that "Rule Number Twenty One stated that the male gender was *more comprehensive* than the female." This rule was followed 100 years later by "the 1850 Act of Parliament which legally insisted that *he* stood for *she.*" See *Man Made Language,* 148, 150.

13. Cheris Kramarae and Paula Treichler, eds., *A Feminist Dictionary,* 249–250.

14. Adrienne Rich, "The Burning of Paper instead of Children," in *The Fact of a Doorframe: Poems Selected and New 1950–1984,* 117.

15. Although this discussion draws on the original sources, I first encountered muted group theory in two other works which provide useful discussions of its relationship to language: Cheris Kramarae, *Women and Men Speaking;* and Spender, *Man Made Language.*

16. Shirley Ardener, "Introduction," in *Perceiving Women,* ed. Shirley Ardener, viii.

17. Ibid., xv.

18. Ibid., xii.

19. Rachel Blau DuPlessis, *Writing beyond the Ending: Narrative Strategies of Twentieth-Century Women Writers,* 41.

20. Tillie Olsen, *Silences;* and Joanna Russ, *How to Suppress Women's Writing.*

21. Joni Seager and Ann Olson, *Women in the World: An International Atlas,* map 24. Seager and Olson report:

> Adults who can neither read nor write also cannot participate fully in modern life. More adult women than men fall into this category: two-thirds of the world's illiterates are women; in seventeen countries over 90 per cent of women are illiterate.
>
> This is largely the legacy of women's relative confinement to domestic and private life, and the widespread prejudice against educating girls.
>
> Almost everywhere the gap in literacy between women and men is widening. This is especially true in cities, where men have more opportunities—often at work—to learn to read and write. So, while literacy for both women and men is higher in cities than in rural areas, urbanization more often than not leaves women at a relative disadvantage. Women's illiteracy is also more hidden than men's, and official figures are known to underestimate the problem.

22. Catherine MacKinnon provides a blistering articulation of the power dynamics that have silenced women: ". . . when you are powerless, you don't just speak differently. A lot, you don't speak. Your speech is not just differently articulated, it is silenced. Eliminated, gone. You aren't just deprived of a language with which to articulate your distinctiveness, although you are; you are deprived of a life out of which articulation might come. Not being heard is not just a function of lack of recognition, not just that no one

knows how to listen to you, although it is that; it is also silence of the deep kind, the silence of being prevented from having anything to say" (*Feminism Unmodified: Discourses on Life and Law*, 39).

23. Marilyn Frye analyzes this problem:

> Reading or hearing the speeches of men on the unintelligibility of women, I imagine the men are like people who for some reason can see everything but automobiles and are constantly and painfully perplexed by blasts and roars, thumps and bumps, which they cannot avoid, control or explain. . . . The phallocratic scheme does not admit women as authors of perception, as seers. Man understands his own perception as simultaneously generating and being generated by a point of view. Man is understood to author names; men have a certain status as points of intellectual and perceptual origin. Insofar as the phallocratic scheme permits the understanding that women perceive at all, it features women's perceptions as passive, repetitive of men's perception, non-authoritative. Aristotle said it outright: Women are rational, but do not have authority. (*The Politics of Reality: Essays in Feminist Theory*, 165)

24. Elaine Showalter, "Feminist Criticism in the Wilderness," in *The New Feminist Criticism: Essays on Women, Literature, and Theory*, 262.

25. DuPlessis, *Writing beyond the Ending*, 42.

26. DuPlessis cites W. E. B. DuBois (*The Souls of Black Folk*, 1903) as the originator of this term: "It is a peculiar sensation, the double-consciousness, this sense of always looking at one's self through the eyes of others, of measuring one's soul by the tape of a world that looks on in amused contempt and pity. One ever feels his twoness—an American, a Negro; two souls, two thoughts, two unreconciled strivings; two warring ideals in one dark body, whose dogged strength alone keeps it from being torn asunder" (cited in ibid., 208).

27. Spender, *Man Made Language*, 102. Spender notes that the speed with which women are moving out of our muted state caused her some concern while she worked on her book: "In some cases women were moving so quickly away from their muted state that in typical 'academic' style I was concerned that I would not be able to document sufficiently some of the examples of women's language which I was seeking" (105).

28. See Hélène Cixous, "The Laugh of the Medusa," in *New French Feminisms*, ed. Elaine Marks and Isabelle de Courtivron, 251; Adrienne Rich, "Motherhood: The Contemporary Emergency and the Quantum Leap," in *On Lies, Secrets, and Silence*, 259–260; and Mary Daly, *Beyond God the Father: Toward a Philosophy of Women's Liberation*, 8.

29. Adrienne Rich, "Transcendental Etude," in *The Fact of a Doorframe*, 268.

30. Cynthia Enloe, "Fawn Hall and Betsy North Revisited," *Sojourner* 13 (December 1987): 13. Kramarae and Treichler, *A Feminist Dictionary*, 438,

quote Laura J. Lederer, ed., *Take Back the Night* (New York: William Morrow, 1980), 19, in their "Take Back the Night" entry: "A slogan 'first used in the United States as a theme for a national protest march down San Francisco's pornography strip. The march took place at night and was in the spirit of many similar events taking place all over the world. Take Back the Night was a profound symbolic statement of our commitment to stopping the tide of violence against women in all arenas, and our demand that perpetrators of such violence—from rapists to batterers to pornographers—be held responsible for their actions and made to change.'"

31. DuPlessis, *Writing beyond the Ending*, 41.

32. Alicia Suskin Ostriker, *Stealing the Language: The Emergence of Women's Poetry in America*, 92.

33. Adrienne Rich, "Power and Danger: Works of a Common Woman," in *On Lies, Secrets, and Silence*, 247.

1. This Narrow Language

1. Lidoff, "Clearing Her Throat," 23.

2. Germaine Greer, *The Female Eunuch*, 41, cited in Spender, *Man Made Language*, 177.

3. Although the current wave of feminism did not provide the first critique of male dominance, the fact remains that in the fifties and sixties earlier critiques had been thoroughly suppressed and the contemporary women's movement did not yet exist.

2. Illuminating the Dark Lives of Women

1. Hulley, "Interview with Grace Paley," 27.

2. Ferdinand de Saussure, *Course in General Linguistics*, ed. Charles Bally and Albert Sechehaye, 114.

3. Jacques Derrida, *Positions*, trans. and annotated Alan Bass, 24.

4. Mikhail Bakhtin, *The Dialogic Imagination*, ed. Michael Holquist, trans. Caryl Emerson and Holquist, 293.

5. Margaret Homans, *Bearing the Word: Language and Female Experience in Nineteenth-Century Women's Writing*, 33.

6. Toril Moi, *Sexual/Textual Politics: Feminist Literary Theory*, 136.

7. Dale M. Bauer, *Feminist Dialogics: A Theory of Failed Community*, 167.

8. I first labeled the silencing of women produced by male-dominated language as "distortions," but that didn't seem to name the problem adequately. Pauline Bart suggested the phrase "denials and distortions."

9. Sara Maitland, in *Why Children?* ed. Stephanie Dowrick and Sibyl Grundberg (London: Women's Press, 1980), 88, cited in Kramarae and Treichler, *A Feminist Dictionary*, 349.

10. Daly, *Beyond God the Father,* 8.

11. Monique Wittig, *Les Guérillères,* cited in Xavière Gauthier, "Is There Such a Thing as Women's Writing?" in *New French Feminisms,* ed. Marks and de Courtivron, 163.

12. Kramarae and Treichler, *A Feminist Dictionary,* includes these and thousands of other words either invented or defined from a woman-centered perspective.

13. Lawrence Crawford, "Victor Shklovskij: *Différence* in Defamiliarization," *Comparative Literature* 36 (Summer 1984): 209–219.

14. Ibid., 210.

15. Wendy Smith, "PW Interviews Grace Paley," *Publishers Weekly,* April 5, 1985, 72.

16. Hulley, "Interview with Grace Paley," 24.

17. Taylor, "Grace Paley on Storytelling and Story Hearing," 52.

18. Reading Psalm 8:4–8 from a feminist perspective, one cannot help but note its glorification of man and male dominance: "What is man, that thou art mindful of him? and the son of man that thou visitest him? For thou hast made him a little lower than the angels, and hast crowned him with glory and honour. Thou madest him to have dominion over the works of thy hands; thou hast put all things under his feet: all sheep and oxen, yea, and the beasts of the field; the fowl of the air, and the fish of the sea, and whatsoever passeth through the paths of the seas."

19. Edward Said, *Beginnings: Intention and Method,* 34.

20. Luce Irigaray, *Speculum of the Other Woman,* trans. Gillian C. Gill, especially 294–304. Comments from Betsy Draine helped me to see these connections.

21. Adrienne Rich, "Natural Resources," in *The Fact of a Doorframe,* 264.

22. Lidoff, "Clearing Her Throat," 13.

23. Virginia Woolf, *Orlando,* 219.

24. Karen Endor and Naomi Thiers, "We're Talking to Each Other More and More: An Interview with Grace Paley," *Off Our Backs* 18 (April 1988): 4.

25. Ibid.

26. Smith, "PW Interviews Grace Paley," 72.

27. Richard Madsen Bellah, William M. Sullivan, Ann Swidler, and Steven M. Tipton, *Habits of the Heart: Individualism and Commitment in American Life,* vii, echoes Paley's critique of the limits of individualism: "It seems to us that it is individualism, and not equality, as Tocqueville thought, that has marched inexorably through our history. We are concerned that this individualism may have grown cancerous—that it may be destroying those social integuments that Tocqueville saw as moderating its more destructive potentialities, that it may be threatening the survival of freedom itself."

28. Smith, "PW Interviews Grace Paley," 72.

29. Ibid.

3. What Is There to Laugh?

1. For a thorough discussion of these factors and their relationship to women's mutedness, see Cheris Kramarae, "Joking Matters," in *Women and Men Speaking*, 52–63.

2. Gloria Kaufman, "Introduction," in *Pulling Our Own Strings: Feminist Humor and Satire*, ed. Gloria Kaufman and Mary Kay Blakely, 14.

3. Kate Clinton, "Making Light: Another Dimension: Some Notes on Feminist Humor," *Trivia* 1 (Fall 1982): 39.

4. Kramarae (*Women and Men Speaking*) is one of numerous researchers who have begun to describe women's alternative tradition. Even when women participate in a form of humor more characteristic of the male tradition (i.e., joke-telling), we still maintain a separate tradition. In a comparison of the male and female joke-telling traditions, Carol Mitchell collected a total of 1,507 jokes. She found that male joke-telling sessions are competitive, with each man attempting to tell a funnier joke than the last. Even when women are audience members at such sessions, they usually do not participate, preferring to use jokes to conciliate opposing views. Further, women tell jokes that are less openly aggressive, and they are more likely to tell those jokes in private rather than public settings. Whereas men are confident telling jokes to large groups and to strangers, women prefer small groups of close friends. Finally, Mitchell found that women place less value on joke-telling than men do, so that jokes in women's groups function as a minor part of the conversation, while in men's groups they tend to become an end in themselves ("Some Differences in Male and Female Joke-Telling," in *Women's Folklore, Women's Culture*, ed. R. A. Jordan and S. J. Kalcik, 163–186).

5. See ibid. for a discussion of private versus public settings. For the characteristics of the female tradition, see Mary Crawford, "Humor in Conversational Context: Beyond Biases in the Study of Gender and Humor," in *Representations: Social Constructions of Gender*, ed. R. K. Unger.

6. M. Jenkins, "What's So Funny? Joking Among Women," in *Proceedings of the First Berkeley Women and Language Conference*, ed. S. Bremner, N. Caskey, and B. Moonwomon (Berkeley: University of California at Berkeley, 1985), cited in Crawford, "Humor in Conversational Context."

7. Clinton, "Making Light," 38–39.

8. Marianne DeKoven, "Mrs. Hegel-Shtein's Tears," *Partisan Review* 68, no. 2 (1981): 221.

9. Anne Tyler, "Mothers in the City," *New Republic* 192, no. 7 (April 29, 1985): 39.

10. Taylor, "Grace Paley on Storytelling and Story Hearing," 56.

11. My thoughts about this distinction were clarified by hearing Nancy Walker discuss the differences between the motives of male and female humorists. She noted that both point to social incongruity and attempt to restore balance. But the male locates reason and right in himself, while the

female locates incongruity in herself—she's out of step (Nancy Walker, "Inescapable Stereotypes? Protest and Perpetuation" [paper delivered at the National Women's Studies Association Convention, Seattle, Washington, June 1985]). She develops these ideas in "Feminist Humor," in *A Very Serious Thing: Women's Humor and American Culture,* esp. 139–145.

12. Ostriker, *Stealing the Language,* 201.

13. See also the discussion of the "give me another globe" joke below.

14. See chapter 4 for a full discussion of the way this story functions as a critique of Paley's writing.

15. Bonetti, *American Audio Prose Library Interview.*

16. "Hilarious" might seem an overstatement to some readers of Paley. Yet when (on several occasions) I have read portions of the two previous chapters to groups, Paley's redefinitions have produced hearty laughter. Humor seems to work best in a communal setting. Where an audience bursts into laughter, a silent reader will merely smile.

17. Adrienne Rich, "Disloyal to Civilization: Feminism, Racism, Gynephobia," in *On Lies, Secrets, and Silence,* 275–310.

18. Ostriker, *Stealing the Language,* 168.

19. These definitions appear in *Webster's New 20th Century Dictionary, Unabridged* (Cleveland: World Publishing Company, 1970) and *Webster's New Collegiate Dictionary* (Springfield, Mass.: G. & C. Merriam Company, 1976).

20. ". . . as we consulted dictionaries and thesauruses, we found that words describing women ultimately led to the description 'prostitute.'" *Feminist English Dictionary: An Intelligent Woman's Guide to Dirty Words* (Chicago: Loop Center YWCA, 1973), cited in Kramarae, *Women and Men Speaking,* 42–43.

21. Walker, *A Very Serious Thing,* 126–129.

22. Ostriker, *Stealing the Language,* 168.

23. Ibid., 200.

24. DeKoven, "Mrs. Hegel-Shtein's Tears," 221.

25. Taylor, "Grace Paley on Storytelling and Story Hearing," 56–57.

26. Walker, *A Very Serious Thing,* 115.

27. Leo Rosten, *The Joys of Yiddish,* xxiv.

4. Not Necessarily the End

1. DuPlessis, *Writing beyond the Ending,* 3.

2. Ibid.

3. Ibid., 5.

4. At the beginning of *Enormous Changes at the Last Minute,* Paley includes this note: "Everyone in this book is imagined into life except the father. No matter what story he has to live in, he's my father, I. Goodside, M.D., artist, and storyteller."

5. Lidoff, "Clearing Her Throat," 18.

6. Hulley, "Interview with Grace Paley," 33–34.

7. In Lidoff, "Clearing Her Throat," 19–20, Paley discusses another aspect of this story, not considered in this analysis:

> The story's about a couple of things. It's about story telling, but it's also really about generational attitudes towards life, and it's about history. I tend not to look at things psychologically so much, but historically, I think. And for him, he was quite right, from his point of view. He came from a world where there *was* no choice, where you couldn't really decide to change careers when you were forty-one years old, you know. You couldn't decide to do things like that. Once you were a junkie, that was the end of everything. Once you were anything, that was it. Who you were was what you were. And she was speaking really from her own particular historical moment, and in another country besides, where things were more open. . . . I mean she really lives at a time when things have more open possibility, and for a group or a class that had more possibilities and a generation in that line, because he was an immigrant and he just about got here and did all right by the skin of his teeth. So she was really speaking for people who had more open chances.

8. This connection is explored by Sandra M. Gilbert and Susan Gubar, *The Madwoman in the Attic: The Woman Writer and the Nineteenth-Century Literary Imagination,* 14.

9. DuPlessis, *Writing beyond the Ending,* 178.

10. At one point, having observed that characters sometimes fail to conform to the author's expectations, the daughter in "A Conversation" explains that in such cases "you just have to let the story lie around till some agreement can be reached between you and the stubborn hero" (164). Such a respect for the autonomy and independent life of her characters stands in marked contrast to the notions of paternity and ownership characteristic of dominant texts. Gilbert and Gubar note:

> That such a notion of "ownership" or possession is embedded in the metaphor of paternity leads to yet another implication of this complex metaphor. For if the author/father is owner of his text and of his reader's attention, he is also, of course, owner/possessor of the subjects of his text, that is to say of those figures, scenes, and events—those brain children—he has both incarnated in black and white and "bound" in cloth and leather. Thus, because he is an *author,* a "man of letters" is simultaneously, like his divine counterpart, a father, a master or ruler, and an owner: the spiritual type of a patriarch, as we understand that term in Western society. (*The Madwoman in the Attic,* 7)

11. DuPlessis, *Writing beyond the Ending,* 151.
12. Jane Miller, *Women Writing about Men,* 2.
13. DuPlessis, *Writing beyond the Ending,* 4.

14. Hulley, "Interview with Grace Paley," 28.

15. Chapter 6, "Voices from Who Knows Where," returns to this issue of alternate points of view on the same story.

16. Judith Arcana, "Introductory Headnotes for 'Friends,'" in *Women's Friendship Stories,* ed. Susan Koppelman.

17. Ibid.

5. As Simply as Possible

1. Ostriker notes the gendered nature of critical comments about poets, wherein excellence is described through metaphors of size and force, "great, powerful, forceful, masterly, violent, large," while complimentary adjectives for females shift toward diminutives, "graceful, subtle, elegant, delicate, cryptic, and, above all, modest" (*Stealing the Language,* 3). The same tendency toward a gendered evaluation may exist in the privileging of the novel as the more serious (because larger) literary work.

2. Here are examples of the reviewers' comments, including fuller quotes of the passages in which the preceding remarks appeared:

> Several of the stories in *Enormous Changes at the Last Minute* look under-powered; they present a whimsical mood, or quizzical wisps of an idea or situation which is not always fully rounded or developed. Yet they can scarcely be regarded as long prose poems. They appear rather as imaginative elaborations of notes from a social worker's experience concerning unmarried mothers on relief, junkies, the rape or death of children. (Renee Winegarten, "Paley's Comet," *Midstream* 20 [December 1974]: 66)

> Her tales of woe are short and written within an inch of their lives. . . . While the lives she describes are indeed plain and grim, her telling is insistently unplain, and the effect is to make one remember sentences—their place in a paragraph even, or on the page—rather than the lives of people. The individual tales meld and blur into each other, because Paley works too hard, I think, at the wrong things. (Roger Sale, *Hudson Review* 27 [Winter 1974–75]: 629–630)

> The plotting in *Enormous Changes* ranges from the incredibly bad to the nonexistent, and the reader often gets the feeling that the author found herself in the middle of a story and then simply ran out of the imaginative energy necessary to complete it. (Jane Larkin Crain, "Ordinary Lives," *Commentary* 58, no. 1 [July 1974]: 92–93)

> "Gloomy Tune" . . . ends so abruptly it almost skids off the page. . . . "Living" and "The Burdened Man" hardly have a chance to get airborne before they end with a wry thump. . . . Good as the present collection is, however, I suspect that its unevenness reflects the fact that during these past years

she must often have felt that her attentions were needed in places far from her typewriter. (Lis Harris, "New Yorkers That Sound Like New Yorkers," *New York Times Book Review,* March 17, 1974, 3)

Her writerly gifts are for naturalism, not for surrealism or the symbolic, and such tales as "At That Time, or the History of a Joke," "In the Garden," and "This Is a Story about My Friend George, the Toy Inventor" become little more than nervous, haphazard sketches about ill-defined people—they neither move in the quick, suprising circle of a good parable nor loft the mundane up into the heights of sunny metaphor. (Michiko Kakutani, *New York Times,* April 10, 1985, C20)

The half-dozen very short stories (two to five pages long) Miss Paley has included in *Later the Same Day* don't work. They seem pat, offering quick bits of insight in clever contexts not developed enough to allow Miss Paley's artistry to shine through. (Robert R. Harris, "Pacifists with Their Dukes Up," *New York Times Book Review,* April 14, 1985, 7)

3. For a fuller discussion, see Taylor, "Grace Paley on Storytelling and Story Hearing," 46–58.

4. Kristin Langellier, "Performing Women's Personal Narratives" (paper presented at Speech Communication Association Convention, Chicago, November 1986), 2–6. Langellier draws these conclusions from a survey of the following sources: K. Baldwin, "Woof! A word on women's roles in family storytelling," in *Women's Folklore, Women's Culture,* ed. R. A. Jordan and S. J. Kalcik (Philadelphia: University of Pennsylvania Press, 1985), 149–162; D. Hall and K. Langellier, "'Is This What You Want to Know?' Women Interviewing Women" (paper presented at the Eastern Communication Association Convention, Atlantic City, New Jersey, May 1986); M. M. Jenkins, "The Story Is in the Telling: A Cooperative Style of Storytelling among Women," In *Gewalt Durch Sprache: Die Vergewaltingung von Fraues in Gesprachen,* ed. S. Tromel-Plotz (Frankfurt am Main: Feisher Taschenbuch Verlag, 1982), ERIC Document Reproduction Service No. ED 238 083; S. Kalcik, ". . . Like Ann's Gynecologist or the Time I Was Almost Raped," in *Women and Folklore,* ed. C. F. Farrer (Austin: University of Texas Press, 1978), 3–11; W. Labov and J. Waletzky, "Narrative Analysis: Oral Versions of Personal Experience," in *Essays on the Verbal and Visual Arts,* ed. J. Helms (Seattle: University of Washington Press, 1967), 12–44; K. M. Langellier and E. E. Peterson, "Spinstorying: A Communication Analysis of Women's Storytelling" (paper presented at the Speech Communication Association Convention, Chicago, November 1984); L. Polanyi, "So What's the Point?" *Semiotica* 25 (1981): 207–241; and J. Robinson, "Personal Narratives Reconsidered," *Journal of American Folklore* 94 (1981): 59–85. See also G. Bennett, "Narrative as Expository Discourse," *Journal of American Folklore* 99 (1986):

415–434; D. Maltz and R. A. Borker, "A Cultural Approach to Male/Female Miscommunication," in *Language and Social Identity,* ed. J. J. Gumperz (Cambridge: Cambridge University Press, 1982), 196–216; and Eric E. Peterson and Kristin M. Langellier, "The Risk of Performing Personal Narratives," in *On Narratives,* ed. H. Geissner (Frankfurt am Main: Scriptor, 1987), 98–115.

5. Lidoff, "Clearing Her Throat," 17.

6. David Hayman and Eric S. Rabkin, *Form in Fiction: An Introduction to the Analysis of Narrative Prose,* 144.

7. Taylor, "Grace Paley on Storytelling and Story Hearing," 47.

8. Hulley, "Interview with Grace Paley," 23.

9. Ibid., 35–36.

10. This comment was quoted on the jacket of the cloth edition of *Enormous Changes at the Last Minute.* It's actually part of a third-person description of Paley captioning her picture, but although the point of view is third person, the prose is clearly recognizable (and acknowledged) as Paley's own: "This is Grace Paley looking better than usual because she's in Karl Bissinger's house, among his green thumbs and in the eye of his camea. She's a New Yorker, and has been a typist, a housewife, and a writer most of her life. Right now she is also a teacher at Sarah Lawrence College. She's a somewhat combative pacifist and cooperative anarchist. She writes short stories because art is too long and life is too short. All of this is fairly accurate because she wrote it."

11. Taylor, "Grace Paley on Storytelling and Story Hearing," 51.

12. Hulley, "Interview with Grace Paley," 20.

13. Ibid., 31.

14. Lidoff, "Clearing Her Throat," 12.

15. In "Documenting Performance Knowledge: Two Narrative Techniques in Grace Paley's Fiction," *Southern Speech Communication Journal* 53 (Fall 1987): 65–79, I discuss how staging "The Immigrant Story" for chamber theater revealed one instance of collaborative narration.

16. Bonetti, *American Audio Prose Library Interview.*

17. Arcana, "Introductory Headnotes for 'Friends.'"

18. The reference seems to be to "Goodbye and Good Luck." Once again, Paley's practice of making extratextual references to her other stories resists closure. It also works in this story, as in "A Conversation with My Father," to suggest that the narrator of this particular story is Paley herself.

19. Hulley, "An Interview with Grace Paley," 38.

20. Lidoff, "Clearing Her Throat," 18.

21. Grace Paley, *365 Reasons Not to Have Another War: Peace Calendar 1989.*

22. Geoffrey H. Hartman, "Introduction," in *Midrash and Literature,* ed. Geoffrey H. Hartman and Sanford Budick, ix–xiii.

23. An earlier draft of this story appears in *Climbing Fences,* ed. Sybil Claiborne (New York: War Resisters League, 1987). This is a booklet pub-

lished to commemorate Paley's sixty-fifth birthday and the sixty-fifth anniversary of the War Resisters League.

24. Lidoff, "Clearing Her Throat," 23.

6. Voices from Who Knows Where

1. This count includes "Politics," a story that uses a first-person pronoun only in the first sentence (see discussion later in this chapter).

2. Even those stories that are apparently third-person often have a first-person narrator embedded in them. For instance, "Politics," a largely third-person account of the political activities of some neighborhood women, begins, "A group of mothers from *our* neighborhood went down to the Board of Estimate Hearing and sang a song" (my emphasis). Those stories that contain no first-person narrative frequently use that close kin of first-person narration, the reflector narrator.

3. It is worth noting that even Paley's third-person narrators speak in a colloquial style and often reflect a particular character's perspective—four are stories about Faith, reflecting her point of view.

4. Taylor, "Grace Paley on Storytelling and Story Hearing," 46–47.

5. Lidoff, "Clearing Her Throat," 7. The third story Paley wrote was "A Woman, Young and Old."

6. Hulley, "Interview with Grace Paley," 29.

7. See the discussion in Spender, *Man Made Language,* 127.

8. Julie R. McMillan, A. Kay Clifton, Diane McGrath, and Wanda S. Gale, "Women's Language: Uncertainty or Interpersonal Sensitivity and Emotionality?" *Sex Roles* 3 (1977): 545–559, cited in Judy C. Pearson, *Gender and Communication,* 189.

9. Lidoff, "Clearing Her Throat," 12.

10. An exact count is difficult because in a few stories it is impossible to determine whether the narrator is Faith or simply someone close to her (and to Paley herself) in age, values, and disposition.

11. Bonetti, *American Audio Prose Library Interview.*

12. Ibid.

13. I first noticed the ambiguous status of Faith's narrative remarks in this passage when directing a chamber theater production of "The Immigrant Story." Because performance demands that we make the time and place of the utterance physical, one cannot perform this passage without confronting the question of whether Faith addresses the reader/audience, Jack, or both. I have described the way performance focuses our attention on this issue in "Documenting Performance Knowledge," 65–79.

14. In "Friends," Ann, Susan, and Faith visit their friend Selena and return home on the train. In "The Expensive Moment," Faith and Ruth have soup together at the Art Foods Deli.

15. Taylor, "Grace Paley on Storytelling and Story Hearing," 53.

Bibliography

Arcana, Judith. "Introductory Headnotes for 'Friends.'" In *Women's Friendship Stories,* edited by Susan Koppelman. Norman: University of Oklahoma Press, forthcoming.

Ardener, Shirley, ed. *Perceiving Women.* London: Malaby Press, 1975.

Bakhtin, Mikhail. *The Dialogic Imagination.* Edited by Michael Holquist and translated by Caryl Emerson and Michael Holquist. Austin: University of Texas Press, 1981.

Bauer, Dale M. *Feminist Dialogics: A Theory of Failed Community.* New York: State University of New York Press, 1988.

Baumback, Jonathan. "Life-Size." Review of *Enormous Changes at the Last Minute* by Grace Paley. *Partisan Review* 42, no. 2 (1975): 303–306.

Bellah, Richard Madsen, William M. Sullivan, Ann Swidler, and Steven M. Tipton. *Habits of the Heart: Individualism and Commitment in American Life.* New York: Harper & Row, 1985.

Bonetti, Kay. *American Audio Prose Library Presents an Interview with Grace Paley.* AAPL 6102. Columbia, Mo.: American Audio Prose Library, Inc., 1986. Audio cassette.

Claiborne, Sybil, ed. *Climbing Fences.* New York: War Resisters League, 1987.

Clinton, Kate. "Making Light: Another Dimension: Some Notes on Feminist Humor." *Trivia* 1 (Fall 1982): 37–42.

Crain, Jane Larkin. "Ordinary Lives." Review of *Enormous Changes at the Last Minute* by Grace Paley. *Commentary* 58, no. 1 (July 1974): 92–93.

Crawford, Mary. "Humor in Conversational Context: Beyond Biases in the Study of Gender and Humor." In *Representations: Social Constructions of Gender,* edited by R. K. Unger. Amityville, N.Y.: Baywood Press, forthcoming.

Crawford, Lawrence. "Victor Shklovskij: *Différence* in Defamiliarization." *Comparative Literature* 36 (Summer 1984): 209–219.

Daly, Mary. *Beyond God the Father: Toward a Philosophy of Women's Liberation*. Boston: Beacon Press, 1973.

DeKoven, Marianne. "Mrs. Hegel-Shtein's Tears." *Partisan Review* 68, no. 2 (1981): 217–223.

Derrida, Jacques. *Positions*. Translated and annotated by Alan Bass. Chicago: University of Chicago Press, 1972.

DuPlessis, Rachel Blau. *Writing beyond the Ending: Narrative Strategies of Twentieth-Century Women Writers*. Bloomington: Indiana University Press, 1985.

Endor, Karen, and Naomi Thiers. "We're Talking with Each Other More and More: An Interview with Grace Paley." *Off Our Backs* 18 (April 1988): 4–5.

Enloe, Cynthia. "Fawn Hall and Betsy North Revisited." *Sojourner* 13 (December 1987): 13.

Frye, Marilyn. *The Politics of Reality: Essays in Feminist Theory*. Trumansburg, N.Y.: Crossing Press, 1983.

Gilbert, Sandra M., and Susan Gubar. *The Madwoman in the Attic: The Woman Writer and the Nineteenth-Century Literary Imagination*. New Haven: Yale University Press, 1979.

Harris, Lis. "New Yorkers That Sound Like New Yorkers." Review of *Enormous Changes at the Last Minute*. *New York Times Book Review*, March 17, 1974, 3.

Harris, Robert R. "Pacifists with Their Dukes Up." Review of *Later the Same Day* by Grace Paley. *New York Times Book Review*, April 14, 1985, 7.

Hartman, Geoffrey H., and Sanford Budick, eds. *Midrash and Literature*. New Haven: Yale University Press, 1986.

Hayman, David, and Eric S. Rabkin. *Form in Fiction: An Introduction to the Analysis of Narrative Prose*. New York: St. Martin's Press, 1974.

Homans, Margaret. *Bearing the Word: Language and Female Experience in Nineteenth-Century Women's Writing*. Chicago: University of Chicago Press, 1986.

Hulley, Kathleen. "Interview with Grace Paley." *Delta, revue du Centre d'Étude et de Recherches sur les Écrivains du Sud aux États-Unis* 14 (1982): 19–40.

———. "Introduction: Grace Paley's Resistant Form." *Delta, revue du Centre d'Étude et de Recherches sur les Écrivains du Sud aux États-Unis* 14 (1982): 3–18.

Irigaray, Luce. *Speculum of the Other Woman*. Translated by Gillian C. Gill. Ithaca: Cornell University Press, 1985.

Kakutani, Michiko. Review of *Later the Same Day* by Grace Paley. *New York Times*, April 10, 1985, C20.

Kaufman, Gloria. "Introduction." In *Pulling Our Own Strings: Feminist Humor and Satire*, edited by Gloria Kaufman and Mary Kay Blakely. Bloomington: Indiana University Press, 1980.

Kramarae, Cheris. *Women and Men Speaking.* Rowley, Mass.: Newbury House Publishers, 1981.

Kramarae, Cheris, and Paula Treichler, eds. *A Feminist Dictionary.* Boston: Pandora Press, 1985.

Langellier, Kristin. "Performing Women's Personal Narratives." Paper presented at Speech Communication Association Convention, Chicago, November 1986.

Lidoff, Joan. "Clearing Her Throat: An Interview with Grace Paley." *Shenandoah* 32, no. 3 (1981): 3–26.

MacKinnon, Catherine. *Feminism Unmodified: Discourses on Life and Law.* Cambridge, Mass.: Harvard University Press, 1987.

Marks, Elaine, and Isabelle de Courtivron. *New French Feminisms.* Boston: University of Massachusetts Press, 1980.

Miller, Jane. *Women Writing about Men.* New York: Pantheon Books, 1986.

Mitchell, Carol. "Some Differences in Male and Female Joke-Telling." In *Women's Folklore, Women's Culture,* edited by R. A. Jordan and S. J. Kalcik. Philadelphia: University of Pennsylvania Press, 1985.

Moi, Toril. *Sexual/Textual Politics: Feminist Literary Theory.* London: Methuen, 1985.

Novak, William. "The Uses of Fiction: To Reveal and to Heal." Review of *Enormous Changes at the Last Minute* by Grace Paley. *America,* June 8, 1974, 459–460.

Olsen, Tillie. *Silences.* New York: Dell Publishing, 1978.

Ostriker, Alicia Suskin. *Stealing the Language: The Emergence of Women's Poetry in America.* Boston: Beacon Press, 1986.

Paley, Grace. *Enormous Changes at the Last Minute.* New York: Farrar, Straus, Giroux, 1974.

———. "Introduction to 'A Conversation with My Father.'" In *Fathers: Reflections by Daughters,* edited by Ursula Owen. New York: Pantheon Books, 1985.

———. *Later the Same Day.* New York: Farrar, Straus, Giroux, 1985.

———. *The Little Disturbances of Man: Stories of Women and Men at Love.* New York: Doubleday, 1959; New York: Plume, 1973.

———. *365 Reasons Not to Have Another War: Peace Calendar 1989.* Paintings by Vera B. Williams. Philadelphia: New Society Publishers, 1989.

Pearson, Judy C. *Gender and Communication.* Dubuque, Iowa: William C. Brown, 1985.

Rich, Adrienne. *The Fact of a Doorframe: Poems Selected and New 1950–1984.* New York: Norton, 1984.

———. *On Lies, Secrets, and Silence.* New York: Norton, 1979.

Rosten, Leo. *The Joys of Yiddish.* New York: McGraw-Hill, 1968.

Russ, Joanna. *How to Suppress Women's Writing.* Austin: University of Texas Press, 1983.

Said, Edward. *Beginnings: Intention and Method.* New York: Columbia University Press, 1985.

Sale, Roger. Review of *Enormous Changes at the Last Minute* by Grace Paley. *Hudson Review* 27 (Winter 1974–75): 629–630.

Saussure, Ferdinand de. *Course in General Linguistics.* Edited by Charles Bally and Albert Sechehaye with the collaboration of Albert Riedlinger, translated and annotated by Roy Harris. LaSalle, Ill.: Open Court, 1986.

Seager, Joni, and Ann Olson. *Women in the World: An International Atlas.* New York: Simon and Schuster, 1986.

Showalter, Elaine. "Feminist Criticism in the Wilderness." In *The New Feminist Criticism: Essays on Women, Literature, and Theory.* New York: Pantheon Books, 1985.

Smith, Wendy. "PW Interviews Grace Paley." *Publishers Weekly,* April 5, 1985, 71–72.

Spender, Dale. *Man Made Language.* London: Routledge and Kegan Paul, 1980.

Taylor, Jacqueline. "Documenting Performance Knowledge: Two Narrative Techniques in Grace Paley's Fiction." *Southern Speech Communication Journal* 53 (Fall 1987): 65–79.

———. "Grace Paley on Storytelling and Story Hearing." *Literature in Performance* 7 (1987): 46–58.

Tyler, Anne. "Mothers in the City." Review of *Later the Same Day* by Grace Paley. *New Republic* 192, no. 7 (April 29, 1985): 38–39.

Walker, Nancy. *A Very Serious Thing: Women's Humor and American Culture.* Minneapolis: University of Minnesota Press, 1988.

Winegarten, Renee. "Paley's Comet." Review of *Enormous Changes at the Last Minute* by Grace Paley. *Midstream* 20 (December 1974): 65–67.

Woolf, Virginia. *Orlando.* New York: Harcourt Brace Jovanovich, 1928, 1956.

Index

DATE